Hermeneutics of PROMOTION the magic wand to success

Panacea to socio-economic, political, institutional and global development

Amusa Abdulateef

Author of Artisans and artisanship and Being my own boss

Published by Addin Resources Ventures

Ibadan, Nigeria

Copyright: Amusa Abdulateef (2016)

Visit our website www.amusa-abdulateef.com for other books

addinrv@gmail.com   latlib222@yahoo.com

+234 80 5671 0944   +234 80 321 550 18

ISBN:9781979914697

© No part of this book is allowed to be reproduced, stored in a retrieval system or transmitted by any means without the written permission of the author. Violator would face the music accordingly for the infringements on the copyright of the author.

PREFACE

The twin posers that come to mind are 'what do we promote and what is the reason for promotion? Of course, we promote what we know inside out. We promote ideas we desire patronage of. The finished products are promoted to enhance sales. Cultures are promoted to attract other people. We promote a credible aspirant being fielded for a public post. Our individuality, social connections and what we stand for is promoting what we stand for. We are products of a family from an ethnic group practising a religion, belong to one association, have colleagues at schools and always known with certain brands of products and enjoy certain services. We are in short promoting endless things till we bade the world farewell. As a celebrated person, by our speech, our styles of dressing, the endorsements we have of products and services among several others are different ways to announce such items to the world especially to docile buyers for patronage. We promote brands directly and indirectly, voluntarily and involuntarily at a price or no price. We promote to make a new brand to have public awareness and patronage by others. We promote our business, political and social interest. We promote our nation by being good ambassadors, producers of global standard products and services. Through the use or wear of the national insignias, chanting the national anthem and pledge with pride, the hoisting of the national flag, the propagating the policies of government among endless ways are promoting the nation. Preaching one's faith with passion, teaching the good tenets, practicing what we preach and teach, reading the scriptures often at public and private places and promoting one's ethno-religion values with pride are some of the ways of promotion to win more admirers. Political parties promote their ideologies and manifestoes including the celebrated profile of their aspirants. In economic parlance, promotion is a major 'P' among the four marketing mix. The others are product, place and pricing. It is purely an art of showing the stuff an item is made up of to the target people, events, places and institutions for possible patronage. Promotion is done to catch interest and have focus by different institutions. The manufacturers promote products to attract volumes of sales. Many do not know that they promote products, services, institutions, nations, events and several others by their attitudes and hobbies. What we wear promote the designers of the wears, what we eat, drink or consume promote the brands that produce the products; what we sing in songs promote the brand who produced and sang the songs; what we use at homes as gadgets promote the makers to our visitors; the types of cars we ride promote the auto-makers; singing praises of a star is promoting the star. Trooping to stadium to watch a sports club is promoting the club and the competition. Limitless are the ways we promote as free publicists. One can say that promotion is all encompassing. We promote our ethnic through dressing as the cultural values allowed. We promote our religion by walking the talking and valuing the values without shame at all times and places. Political parties promote aspirants and their manifestoes to have landslide victory. Religionist promote their values to retain and win new souls to their faith. We promote the inventions of institutions and nations directly and indirectly, voluntarily and involuntarily. Nations promote the national artefacts to create enabling environments for proliferation of businesses and new investments. There is no limit to what is promoted. Unfortunately, unhealthy promotion is sending many out of business and the dwindling profits. Damsels dress lovely to attract the opposite sex. Shops are painted to create attention from the target visitors who are customers. Workshops are properly organized to create instant love by the prospective clients to bring their problems for fixing. An eligible bachelor must dress smartly always just like the eligible spinsters, they must keep a nice environment where they dwell to send message of being tidy and neat to each other. Accessorizing self, bodies, institutions, environment and packaging that is tune with the vogue in town is a form of promotion. No business would play with manner of providing aesthetics within and around the premises to keep customers coming all the time. If a nation fails to have all working facilities in place, then such has done wrong promotion. And this attitude to the infrastructures would surely tell adversely on the national economy and the living standard of the inhabitants. A school that lacks ambience and serene learning environment with adequate teaching infrastructures, quality and qualified specialized teaching and non-teaching staff members, properly have relevant accreditations from the relevant ministries, departments and agencies has done right promotion that would continually attract enrolment of pupils. Limitless are the ways promotion approach can take across all facets of life. On business, a fact is that all the other P's, of the four marketing mix, must be aggressively and consistently promoted too to enjoy anticipated success. Generally, we are all promoters of different things such as ourselves, our ethnic cultural values, our family lineage, our ties and associations or affiliations, our descendants, our faiths, our town or origin, our nation and national values or heritage, our inventions and others.

In business and economic parlance, it is onus on the entrepreneurs and institutions to design relevant promotion activities for each of the mentioned three other Ps. In an institution, we promote different objects of interests and the objectives or mission plus vision of the institutions. In short, we look beyond the promotion of products, prices and the place (marketplace) but of others like the nation, national values, economic resources, institutions, religion and non-religion, educational and non-educational and of individuals.

Primarily, promotion has to do with placing of direct and indirect adverts in writing or scripting, acting, speech-making, graphics or drawing (visual arts) on right media that would attract target audience. By general study, advertising, in all forms, is a subset of promotion of any socio-economic and political institutions, events, services, business ideas, ethno-religion creed and norms among several others as promotion is all-encompassing.

Towards promoting cherished values of an ethnic, the tenets of a religion, the objective of an organization, mission and vision statement of an institution, the motto of a body, the ideology of a political party, the ruling party agenda promotion among endless things or concepts to promote several measures should be taken and this has been the focus of this book. Our critically analysed findings showed that promotion could also take such forms like praise-singing, folklores, poetry, story, broadcast, campaign. Pen-based professionals like journalists, authors, lawyers, secretaries and broadcasters can negatively or positively create awareness for a product, service, event, institution, government projects, association, ethnic values, religions and all various of disciplines man finds himself. Messages can be passed with right attitudes at the right time. Professional singers and popular thespians could promote certain event, nation, ideology, institution, norm, business et al without taking a dime.

In the book, we assumed that every institution, person, firm, government, ethnic, religion and the likes have either tangible products or visible services to be promoted at all times via the most appropriate popular medium. Many popular artistes voluntary wear certain designers without taking a penny vice versa. Many of the star players and celebrity wear after agreement on the adverts charge with the company being indirectly endorsed. And by the choice of wears or preference by such popular personality in their field of professional specializations, they have promoted the products and the service. Many song-video recorded and block buster films acted at remote villages would at the end popularize the village and villagers as such enters the world map. A white artistes that acted the history of Africans have promoted the negro culture though they earned nothing as revenue for the publicity vice versa. Lodging in a hotel by popular sports idol, thespians, as award venue has popularized such hospitality business. Before you know it, paparazzi has become the order of the day. A logo, motto or complete or incomplete statements on a tee-shirt, jumpsuit, corporate wears, unisex wears could promote designers, films, books, company, institutions and organizations. The writing of preface or foreword of a book by credible author or literary giant, professional literary institutions, associations of authors among others is enough to promote a book into making unprecedented sales in the book market. Imagine the public launching of your product or service by who-is-who in the nation, what a highest level of promotion that would be a commercial success in the market. Products that are sold out at the first few hours or day of formal release has enjoined huge promotion before production. The tickets that have sold out before the kick-off of the soccer contest has enjoined massive promotion before the formal tasks. Signatures popularly referred to as autographs of popular footballers, sportsmen, international singers of repute among others well-loved and followed by millions is enough to create popularity. Watch the footballers in the field of play and meditate over what is written on their jerseys. Such should promote either products or services. Many times the inscription promotes an institution. In the negative side, it could preach hatred for a race. The question in the lip of people who care or the minds who could reflect is 'what does a body language, an inscription, a product jingle, a display, a song, film, the content of a book, the presentations in a documentary, the lengthy preaching on the pulpits... promote? Does it promote brotherliness or division? Does it promote ethnicity or religion bigotry? Nay, some teachings may be misinterpreted for extremism whereas the teachings are fundamentals of the faith.

In short, promotion, in all sense of the word, is like an inevitable and irreplaceable seasoning being a major concept of the four marketing mix. The other P's are the product, the price and the place. The three cannot stand without promotion. If a maker has target classes or segmentations of customers in mind, he must create ways to sell the generic functions of the product to them by the amount it costs in pricing. Business must promote the price via communication to the prospective customers in order to help in planning their finances and other budgets. He, as a producer, must be able to publicize the products by the satisfaction and generic functions before customers could decide to add such into the wish-list and then listed as prioritized list of demands in the market places. And lastly, the point of sales called the outlets where a product so publicized can be picked must be known through public awareness. All these efforts make promotion the salt in the soup. No business, profit or non-profit based, can survive without promotion.

Without mincemeat of words, the major problem facing all entrepreneurs is how to record huge sales. A business that does not have huge number of patronage by demand may never stay afloat. Many makers of products and service providers who fail to recognize the powers of promotion risk longevity in the business environment. Having a good product does not mean attracting automatic patronage. On the other way, having a bad product does not mean a seller would not have huge patronage. In many cases, manufacturers of generic products that could perform the generic functions are not as profitable and popular as products from competitors from outside the shores. What could have rendered products produced within the shores not attracting patronage as the products imported from abroad? It is a fact that the thirst for imported goods may be the reason for this, but not the whole reason. Popularity of product or service may not translate into sales for certain product in a competitive market of substitutes until aggressive pricing and distributional strategies are done.

In retrospect, there are limitless ways to promote one's product, prices, places and others. For instance, a book is promoted by its title and cover-page graphics and artworks plus colours and right captivating fonts. A product can be known and accepted by the packaging of the brand. Good publicist of government must communicate well with the people and foreign nations who are partners to get all supports for its projects. The trademark of a company can promote a product or service. Character of a financier of a politician could promote the candidate just as the party the aspirant belong as a card carrying member. All the instances given got to show that promotion is not a joke in the surviving of all projects not to talk of products and services from business owners and government. Promotion remains the key to a success of all target goals.

In conclusion, limiting our work to how best to promote business outputs- goods and services, towards recording economic growth in the midst of chances of economic recession need all-inclusive strategies. For business to thrive, promotion is in consumption of all locally-made products and patronage of local artisans and other services. By this, wealth is spread as our patriotic attitudes to the preference for the local products at the expense of foreign ones is a form of promotion that is closely related to the nationalistic order. We are all promoters. We promote by our attitudes, profession, qualifications, professional skills and tools, institutions we manage, the positions we hold and limitless ways of creating awareness. All these we may do deliberately or otherwise, for money or charity-based. The author believes that there should be all-encompassing book that would enlighten the public to live a role model as we are promoting certain values, ideology, affiliation, alma mater, associations, products or services one way or the other.

Generally, all things around us are promoting one thing or the other. We are also directly and indirectly promoting everything-idea, cultural values, products, services, institutions, ethnic group, affiliations and the nation with its values. It is not just the sign posts, not just the imprints on advertisement-intent bills and stickers, not just the jingles in radio or the interviews at the tube, everything is promoting a thing. In this book, we expose several ways to promote different persons and institutions beyond the goods and services. In short, author looked beyond the definitions of **PROMOTION** beyond the four marketing mix. Several other issues are treated specially in this highly motivational book "*Hermeneutics of Promotion, the magic wand to success*" that is relevant for:

- a) all producers of products
- b) all service providers
- c) all heads or managers of institutions
- d) all independent marketers and promoters
- e) all sales agents

f) all development of skills
g) all mentors and leaders of thoughts in faiths, business, professional associations, regulatory bodies, political groups and charity-based institutions
h) all motivational speakers and writers
i) all psychologists and sociologists
j) all trainers and coaches.

In view of the preface of the book alone, these facts about promotion comprise:

a) Promoting self especially one's self-worth depicting one's brand before one promotes what one truly stands for
b) Promoting family before promoting your town by their values
c) Promoting the nation before you promote the institutions within
d) Promoting the business before the products and services
e) Promoting quality of the management before the content made up of goods and services
f) Promoting content as you are promoting your station, institution, places, events, nation, faith, associations

Towards achieving the right and target objective or goal, different forms of accessories for promotion depends on the functions of other factors must be done. Let us further look at other comparative instances. School could start promotion during the first time or during the long third term holiday. Proprietor could desire to use the schools where they anticipate pupils as the examination centre. I have seen secondary schools that gave admission forms and conducted the entrance examination in the primary schools where they targeted their pupils for secondary school they were operating. Some prefer to promote their schools by what they have on the media and used the medium to seek admission to their schools.

Invaluable readers, you have a prized asset in the book. The contents shall open the eyes of several individuals and institutions.

DEDICATION

The book is dedicated to my family members and all ardent readers of my works globally.

ACKNOWLEDGEMENT

A million of thanks to the brilliant minds like the director of **Teckmanit technology** in the person of **Mr. Tunde Yusuf** on his encouragements on promotion of my books despite the setbacks from the publishers of my books online. His critics of my works used to bring the better parts of my work. Also, his efforts to promote the preview of one of the intellectual properties in his blog is invaluable. The intellectual contribution of the likes of **Mr. David** and **Mr. Solomon Odekunle** of Supratek Information Consult are not quantifiable. I appreciate the first actor in the show in the person of **Mr. Babatunde Olajide Yusuf** of Omic Technologies. Regards to my inestimable spouse in the person of Kudirah joy Oladipupo and my children, Abdulazeez Ayomide and Sheriffdeen Ayokunmi. I equally thank my in-laws especially Alhaji Bashir Adebisi Oladipupo and his loving wife, Mrs. V.O.A. Adebisi including their children for moral and relentless spiritual supports.

I cannot at any time forget the moral, spiritual and financial contributions of the friends like Olalekan Joel Awujoola, Principal System Analyst Nigerian Defence Academy kaduna; Biodun Tiamiyu Jimoh, ICT expert at Nigerian International School, Benin Republic; Adeolu Ajibade, Ojo Asekhamen, Richard Oyeyiola Oyeyinka, Oseni Jimoh Folayemi, ex-Nulge Chairman Odigbo Local Government; Isiaq Rauf Ademola of Zico Entertainment, Morufah Eniola nee Akanji, Mr. Abubakar Abdurahmon (surveyor) among others.

The confidants like Mr. Alade Babatunde (Dad Farouk), Mr. Muritala Alade, Bro. salaam Abu Salaam (sasco), Muideen Buhari of Mubak wood technology, Abu Rodha, Alhaji Bayo Azeez of Store department, Ministry of Health Oyo State secretariat among others are great in the support and contributions towards my successful writing career.

Lest I forget the brains and minds that brought me up academic-wise in the names of Mrs. Tomilayo Laniya, Proprietress of Bloom Heights Foundation, Mrs. Felicia Modupe Adeleke, Proprietress of Nickdel Groups of Schools, Mr. Bayo Olafusi, Mr Oluwole Fagbola, Mrs. Anike Abe and her hubby, Pastor Abe and their children and Alhaji and Alhaja Rafat Idowu Kunle Sanni for their parental care.

May Almighty reward them abundantly for their invaluable support. I can only say that they are all Godsends who believe in the natural endowments on me from outset.

TABLE OF CONTENT

PREFACE

DEDICATION

ACKNOWLEDGEMENT

CHAPTER ONE

1.1　What does the word 'promotion' mean?

1.2　What do we promote?

1.3　Methods of promotion: How do we promote?

1.4　Channels of promotion: What are the right tracks for promotion? Of what relevance is 'promotion' to any 'business and institution'?

CHAPTER TWO

2.1.　History of promotion

2.2　Promotional strategies in the years past; Promotion strategies in the modern world

CHAPTER THREE

3.1　Promotion and technology

3.2　Promotion and arts

3.3.　Promotion and services

3.4.　Promotion and products

CHAPTER FOUR

What are the gains of promotions to business and institutions? Of what relevance is promotion to a government? What does promotion mean to other facets of live-economy, theology, ideology..?

CHAPTER FIVE

5.1.　What are the challenges facing promotions?

5.2. How best to tackle the challenges headlong?

5.3. What other inputs are needed to improve on promotions?

5.4. Brainstorming general exercises on promotion

CHAPTER SIX

Promotion and political institutions; Promotion and ethno-religion values; Promotion of economic institutions; Promotion and others

EPILOGUE

ABOUT THE BOOK

ABOUT THE AUTHOR

CHAPTER ONE
1.1 WHAT DOES THE WORD 'PROMOTION' MEAN?

Promotion is from the root word '**promote**' which simply means advertise an item through different strategies and channels. We cannot exempt the synonyms words like propagate, display, showcase, upgrade, elevate, enhance, update, endorse, demonstrate, encourage, expose, unveil, accessorize, popularize…as the meanings of the word 'promotion' that is meant to 'invite to buy' for products, 'invite to embrace for faiths', invite to emulate for cultural values and virtuous characters', invite to support in laudable programmes', 'invite to enjoy in services' or 'invite to indulge in developing and growths. Promotions, in any form, are eyes and ears openers, to be aware of apparently hidden things and derivable value attached or added values. One desires to promote good things that would improve one's image in the public and private places. Authors write to promote certain values. Individuals act scripts, written or unwritten to say a lot about races, faiths, associations and status. In dressing codes, certain professions are promoted. Every new item may die the first day of birth unless adequately promoted with right or relevant strategies continually. In short, the relevance or significance of a recommended or carefully packaged idea, accessory, item, product, value, asset, heritage, content, concept and service… to the target consumers or clients (individuals, institutions or governments) must be persistently publicized or created awareness for. In political parlance, the media aides or the public relation officers are promoters of political brands and renowned institutions. The spokespersons of the brands must see it a social duty to engage the public and speak volumes in defence and otherwise on issues related to the person or institution they represent at all times and places. Promotion must not be done at a wide interval of time but at least short time interval if not all periods. This is religiously done via presenting or making useful information available in a very lucid and unambiguous manner with the use of the right medium to create love (instant interest) for patronage by people (customers or clients in businesses), faiths of different faithful and fans from different facets of life. Countless items and styles can be used for promotion. It could be an imposition or by choice. A nation's ministry of education could, by law, force all the printed materials like books, packs of goods, labels on pack or bottle, to have flag of the nation to promote locally made goods. The transport system and practitioners could be 'forced' into the use of certain colours to distinguish cabs from private vehicles. The structures at residential and industrial layouts could be painted with uniform colours as prescribed by the urban departments of the nation. The roads could wear certain paints and landscape to promote the pathways for vehicles and people. If everyone is asked to promote their native culture, they are told to use the costumes, wear the native clothes, use the traditional beads, have traditional hair style, eat traditional food, drink the local drinks, speak the local dialect in communication, use same in business and office interactions, patronize the local artisans and always be proud of everything traditional at the expense of the foreign items. One can imagine the degree of patronage if government uses its influence and powers of controlling all citizens to promote national values and assets (monuments) on the positive development such would bring to the national economic growth and development. Without doubt, this is the first step for a weak economy to regain its strength within a short time. The use of indigenous universally accepted languages to teach pupils in schools would be a better way to discover the local manpower resources aside the promotion of the languages from going extinct (Ref. '**Economic recession, the trends, the causes, the spiral effects and the practicable solutions**' from the same author) Aside the economic gains, there would be tolerating people of different cultural values that would boost social engineering. Individuals and institutions promote one thing or the other. We all stand for something. What we stand for is what we promote directly or indirectly. We promote persons aspiring to become leaders. We promote an office to show what are in place for the occupant and dues. We promote top position and all offices to showcase what is ahead in rewards for the occupants. We promote cultural and national values of a race or races, of tourist places in order to promote proliferation of investments from local and foreign investors. Promotion serves as a form of attraction. Words of ads captures the mood of the people, business, institution or the target to the writers. This reminds me some decades ago when I was a marketing manager of a trading business. We deal with the selling of recharge cards. At first, we locate at strategic point at a safe spot in a T road. We provided attractive aesthetics and settee for those customers that would like to stay for some minutes for calling, meeting and the like. On the advertising board, I used to change the marketing slogan every day. I could recollect some 'those cards you longed for are here'. 'Do not worry to move further in search of cards, they are HERE at cheaper prices'. 'Get your recharge cards at the most affordable prices here now'. It got to an extent that a professional market who used to study different graphics in the attractive variants of letterings being used with the effective use of colour had to shower encomiums on the writer not knowing that the person was me. He asked whether I was a graduate of marketing. Of course, not. But, I am a gifted in terms of marketing goods and services. Another thing I could deduct aside the changing captivation words that would endear people to patronize us is the use of good legible writing that people can see from distance. In the course of this research, I was vindicated as truly attractive letterings attract people into doing business with others. Through the daily activities promoting our products, we moved up from being retailers to wholesalers and we eventually added the selling of virtual cards and mobile phones with subscription identification mobile number cards. Many mobile distributors started to work with us with credit facilities. By the time yours sincerely was leaving the business, a franchise agreement had been signed. At the same time, many who had better advantage and the financial resources use all available channels of communication of what they were selling to pull constantly high crowds of customers. One good thing about promotion is that the more the promotion and its extent via the use of popular medium, the more dynamics introduced into promotion, the more prosperity attracted to the project, place, business, institution among others. Just as the words for promotion are carefully chosen, those who are acting the words must be right item for the promotion. Therefore, several variables must be considered for a promotion to be fruitful. A good promoter must study the actual place to place adverts. If your customers are a particular faith, place your ads and jingles close to the places of worship, meetings and the religious festival periods with the right languages that would show the level of understanding of what your targets are. It is odd for a Muslim school to employ the service of non-Muslims who do not understand what kinds of words to pull the crowds of customers to the school vice versa

In retrospect, promotion is very simple aiming at attracting target clients; if the customers or clients are known by their data and attainments including where they are located. Many applicants fail to endear themselves to their 'employers' simply because of failed self-promotion. Many makers of products and providers of services fail in their bid to woo customers or clients for the use of failed promotional antics. What do I mean? They failed to 'know their customers. Applicants fail to know their boss and the company they applied to. Many proposals are rejected for failure to 'know the clients'. An application that spelt out correctly the addresses of the recipients and correct information about some relevant statistics of the would-be employers shall scale through the first hurdle-consideration for first reading and call for presentation. A seller must also know the resident or location of his customers-to-be. If I intend to sell my book. I must list the would-be buyers who would need the work such as the bookshops, the schools, the libraries, the book retailers or hawkers, the literary agents, the teachers, the mentors, the motivational speakers, the students and the researchers. The next line of action is to select where those are densely populated. If the huge populations are in the central part of America, I would choose the area from my most viable, based on selection on marketing reach and other criteria, digital sellers to send the information about the books to in order to enjoy anticipated huge patronage. Knowing the clients, employers, employees, leaders, geography of a nation, the terrain of an environment, history of a people, the faith of a nation or ethnic group, the major actors in an event and several others is a major strong point very necessary in promotion. An aspirant to a political office must promote self with presentations of actual data of the geographical areas such would be representing. Imagine a candidate that has information about all the institutions, the markets, the private and public institutions, the population by their ideologies, values, faith, interests, their location and other relevant data, the road networks, the sectors among others in the area shall have more acceptability in amassing huge number of votes. No amount of social interactions may do the magic for the aspirants to become a household name. One can see how inevitable and comprehensive promotion is in all facets of life. Many mistakenly equate promotion with advertisement or advertising. Advertising is simply a subset in promotion. Promotion starts from the word go. Advertising is always showing the product, service, event, situation, policy after they have been hatched. Telling people, places, institutions, nations, about a thing before it comes live is promotion. The latter could take all forms including the use of all accessories attached to advertising.

Promotion is a campaign done secretly or openly to create instant awareness in order to create interest. Imagine a headline of a newspaper "**FUTO graduate produced solar-powered tricycle** (vanguard: 2016 Nov 3, page 39). This information has promoted a brand in the electrical/electronic guy, his lecturers and the heads of the department and the faculty, the school where the product was invented, the nation where such feat took place. And this a brand for the nation in the auto-producing industry. Just as the good news branded the listed persons and institutions in a good light, otherwise is the case for bad news from the pen of the writer or the voice of broadcaster in a media station. Manufacturers and service providers must boost the number of interests or likes for their products or services before such business could generate patronage by cash or credit, at the moment or at a later date. A nation whose news journalists report good things about the nation shall enjoy a great boost in tourism and the direct foreign investments for the image laundry with their pens vice versa. It is unpatriotic for a national pressmen be castigating the nation for the hatred they have for the people at the helms. It is right to engage in constructive criticism. Studies showed that those who criticize are found incapable to walk the talk. Instead of discouraging those at the echelons, a critical assessment of how they have gone to balance the story is needed than negative criticism without proffering simple solutions. On my part, I used to read what leaders are doing right and those on the wrong side. With the analyses, I tried to find those areas assistance is needed and I research into practicable solutions that would be packaged and sent to the right offices. This is a way of promoting the nation to greater heights from the low. The same is applicable to all professionals especially those who are most popular in the entertainment world. Let us look at a few illustrations. A school is located at a serene environment conducive to learning. The school is adequately equipped with modern educational materials and staffed with professional and seasoned teachers with success stories in the field. In the jingles, advertisements promote the quality of the school. Also available are sports facilities, Information and Communication Technology department with all sorts of gadgets for the users among other facilities. With all these, the school already has started to promote itself with all the structures and infrastructures in place. Yet, many would-be students may need to be informed before enrolment could be massive. To achieve the target level of enrolment, the school has a big electronic billboard at the front of the school and a junction to the school. It also pays for some adverts on a radio station. In another school whose educational facilities are not up to the former, but the management invests its resources in radio and television station, engages in house to house, market to market, office to office and place of worship to place of worship promotion of the school, such would have massive enrolment within a short time.

Campaign as a promotion takes a lifetime thinking and always dynamic with the dictates of time and event. Sometimes, the mood of people should be considerable factor before a promotion is done for a product, a service, an event, a place, an institution, a policy among others to create awareness as speculated.

Speak your language and never be ashamed at home and public places, make the dialect a major course at schools in order to be close to your cultural values, use the language to take difficult subjects and courses to develop quality manpower, dress your native wears, patronize the local goods and services, eat your local foods and drinks provided they are not contaminants and intoxicating and by these promote your culture. Listening to the local songs; brand the songs, folklores and poetry; brand the clothing, brand the raw materials, brand the professional services, create films and documents from the history. Brand the foods and drinks to meeting exporting standard. Tell and act the real stories showing the historical pasts of the ancient towns, brave warriors, legacies of the past heroes and heroines, recommend locally written books at schools, patronize the schools and hospitals within. Turn the nation into production-based to fast-track service-oriented, tourist-focused, trade-oriented (of retail and wholesale) to boost all the sectors of the economy. All these are ways of **promoting** the invaluable natural assets. In many cases, the baptismal names or the trademark name of a business, the title of a product and others could turn the table for a business. Attractive names could entice lovers and patronage of services. It could open windows of success for business vice versa. Customers are irrational in the market. What attracts some customers may repel others.

Promoting parents all forms of choice advertisements on all available medium. It is a fact that promotion starts from day one even before a product or service is completed. Announcing a product or service before it comes a reality is promotion. Pregnancy announces into the world the coming of a child or children. Every task or union heralds another task or products. This is done to create suspense. Imagine a book that is said to be released soon is promoting the book before its official selling. The previews and reviews of books before release are also a form of promotion. Interviews about events promote the events prior to the d-day. Jingles and analyses of products or services, bouts or sporting activities promote the events. Films premier is another form of promoting the content of tube business. It is right to announce a product, service, event.. before its official release to the target market. I have been a support of publishers and authors who place their intellectual property works on blogs and independent sites before release. Government creation of awareness for an on-coming policies would attract reactions for the better formulation of such policies. It is unfair for imposition of policies as users would see it as dictatorial. In short, with promotion by different means and channels, such event, material would be a sell-out.

In the world of internet-based innovations, promotion can start with the use of short message services, bulk short message services, the instant message services with the use of popular social media handle sites like instagram, facebook, linkedin and twitter among others. I tried to create moments in my twitter account in order to promote my personality as an author. I participated in several phone in or text in programmes in order to enjoy promotion. Names of radio contributions on phone-in documentaries swell to the extent that their connections form fans base for different concepts. Promoting is preparing the minds of the target customers ahead the formal release.

Many film producers used to use certain hotels, schools, the consumption of certain drinks and beverages or even be part of the reference in the mouths of the thespians in order to announce and endorse the products or services to the world. Whenever a star or popular figure wears certain designs with their logo or trademarks, he has indirectly promoted the wears to the public. It is a way of endorsement by the huge-following personality for the item. Imagine the use of items by the socialites, the political figures, the celebrated professionals, the reverent institutions and associations. They have promoted the item! A logo that a product or service is a partner for an event is an endorsement.

Visit stadium especially during live matches, you would notice the running adverts on the walls surrounding the pitch. The makers and the promoter of the jersey, the kits put on, the lights, the pre-match displays, the rewards at stake for all the winners, the pre-match interviews by the competing teams. All these are parts of promotion of the football contest. The proprietors could add more value chains that would attract fans to trickle in droves to the stadium. The arrangement of coloured seats, the light sound at action-packed period and the displays of skills of the teams on the pitch are all forms of promotion. In some other sports, there are street parades and other activity to promote in order to sell out the tickets before the competitions.

In short, limitless is the way promotion is done to catch attention of prospective customers of goods and patronages of services, fans to stadiums, audience to gathering, electorates to the polling station, patients to health facilities, pupils to schools, damsels to beauty salon, fashion designer, visual artists to exhibitions, spectators to stadiums and cinemas, tourists to tourist places and relaxation gardens and parks, patronage at galleries and workshops, trooping for transactions at marketplaces among others. A fact is that 'what attracts individual person, institution, association differ.

Every good news about a company, an individual, an ethnic group, a religion organization, an association, an institution, the nation and the world in general promote policies about the list vice versa. A bad egg in a family has promoted the family in a bad light vice versa. A successful guru in sport has promoted the image of the nation. Imagine the Olympic medal winners, they have shown the nations of the world about their nations. They made their nations the cynosure of all eyes of investors and tourists to attract forex and grow the economies of their nations. I could recall when yours sincerely became one of the winners of an essay competition organized by a popular brand. The school management saw it as a good promotion strategy for the names of the school to appear in the records of the brand and the association of dental therapists in the nation. In the words of the announcer of the prizes, *"if there were no the likes of the reggae star Bob Nesta Marley, who would have known about the big mountains of Jamaica"*. A company makes its policy known through public presentations, unveiling of product or service, official launching and commissioning among others. Many use street entertainers and parades through the nooks and corners to announce the service or the product. Aesthetics for an office could generate attractions. The well-dressed or corporately dressed staff of a company, an institution, an organization could promote the values and mission of such. I have seen people who confessed that the way the state law enforcement agents dress in their uniforms attracted them into joining the forces, I mean the dress code. Kindness of certain professionals in the course of performing their duties create interests in young chaps to adopt the courses towards becoming like them. This is what we tagged as emulating a role model. Designers wear what they design; the beverage makers drink their products; the hairdressers wear different hairstyles to sell and promote their art; the shoes sellers and makers wear shoes to promote what they do in business;.. In short, what a professional used to use is what they sell or trying to promote directly and indirectly.

In view of the discussions, the titles, baptismal or nickname, of an individual, an institution, a nation, an event, a show..... is a form of promotion. The price tag on a product is informing the buyers about how much to pay. An information being passed directly and indirectly is another form of promotion. A baby that grows to become a professional after schooling has added values to his name to earn deserved respect. Simply say, promoting or promotion is inexhaustible in definition. We have thrown open the broader definitions of promotion to all minds to pave the way for other areas under the topic.

1.2   WHAT DO WE PROMOTE?

"We promote self
We promote values
We promote our faiths
We promote our ethnics
We promote our civilization
We promote our institutions
Personalize it thus 'What do I promote?"

Having established the inevitability of promotion, the next poser is the theme '<u>what do we or I promote?</u>' In short, knowingly and unknowingly with different strategies and styles, <u>we promote everything</u> that are valuable to us. By 'us', we mean self, others, family, groups, institutions, towns, nations and the world at large. Such promotion is best done for items, ideas and others that are of quality and everything promotes us by adding values to our persons and personality, institution and the family, ethnic and religion. Otherwise, none is ready to be associated (identified) with wrong things that would incriminate us. We, therefore in essence, promote good virtues always vice versa depending on the blocs we belonged, dream to belong or ascribed or plan to ascribe to in affiliations. If someone likes a football club, he would like to be wearing their jerseys to any place. If someone is interested in a maker, such would equip his house and offices with the items with the engraved names of such thing. We directly promote our faith, personality or brand, our products and services, our family and race, our nation and affiliations. Everyone, who has good name to protect and desires to be a model, takes a pride with good things of life that can add values to better the standard of living. Everyone desires to be known with good names and revered for dignity. Success is everybody's kinsmen but not for failure. Therefore, we all desire to be among the good people who are successful in their trades, ambitions, ideology, institutions. We would prefer to be part and parcel and would therefore proudly promote the ethics and values of each of them. The deviants promote vicious acts. And all the promoters of all forms of criminalities must be attacked with the greater promotion of right acts that would annul the evils. In the incorruptible scriptures, it is revealed **"Ye are the best of people evolved for mankind…. Enjoin righteousness and forbid evils"**. This confirms the mandatory social responsibility placed by the almighty on all believers. And the main reason for this natural responsibility is to rid the earth of evils from people to people, institution to institution and nation to nation. According to the renowned King of England during the world war period *"let each family protect his own family and Britain is safe from attackers"*. This established the relevance of promotion as a responsibility over all human beings no matter the status and position.

By the word 'we', it stands for individuals by their status, affiliations, associations, natural instincts and assets, institutions and their cardinal programmes and projects, ethnic groups and their values, governments' institutions and their policies, employers and the companies under their control, association, professional bodies and what they stand for, producers of goods and service providers. Students can promote their brilliance by entering into contests. I could recall that yours sincerely entered a secondary essay competition in the name of the alma mater. And the prizes won exposed (promoted) the school in the map of the schools that had good essayists in history. Someone who has skills could join the stars at training grounds to hone their skills. Designers enter into exhibitions and trade fairs to exhibit their talents. Cultural ambassadors sensitize the national and international community on the use of indigenous languages for the teaching of the pupils at school in order to have excellent results in external examinations. In Nigeria, **Prof. Babatunde Aliyu Fafunwa**, former minister of Education under **Ibrahim Babangida** military regime proposed the use of indigenous languages to teach the pupils core subjects in the school. Some houses of assemblies in the states clamoured for the use of indigenous dialect for communication in the assemblies in order to promote the languages from going into extinction. Many a tourist attraction places are promoted to the levels of becoming recognized wonders of the world. Parents are usually proud to promote the brilliance and intelligence in their children. Such child is given the best of education and educational-enhanced supports to excel. Writer of potentially popular titles in books is always proud to promote his intellectual property. Natives who are proud of their cultural values and norms use all in their capacity to promote them to other ethnic groups for possible adoption. When the native dress makers export their products to other nations; it is not for profit-making alone but to showcase their traditional clothing. A jobless person should promote his skills; such should hawk his quality from the area of qualifications to all places. It is not limited to the professional circle alone. We have witnessed jobless architect by educational training that joined the labourers of a builder who was discovered at a building site. As taught in the book 'Jobs with zero capital', we taught the readers on how to be at the right places where their innate skills and inherent ability are urgently in hot demands. Those who have football skills should join trainings and probably contests at stadium during the time the coaches and trainers of existing clubs could discover their talents. It is not necessary for a maker of product to outsource for marketers. Hairdressers used to plait hairs or put wigs on dolls for displaying their artistry to would-be customers. Use your product and potential customers would seek for them. Summarily, we promote what will add values to life, what we add spices to living, what will motivate and activate people and institutions to work, what will enhance effectiveness and efficiency in form of tools, what would remove dullness, depression and energize life in all facets, what would build greater personality, what provides aesthetics.

Think of anything that can influence positively or negatively in all the environments, we intentionally or otherwise promote by all parts of our body, our office, our homes, our faith places, our immovable and movable assets among others through the use of the most affordable, available and the widest reach medium. Our skills and inherent traits promote our person. Our frame shows our personality. How we behave portrays us either in good or bad light. The quality of jobs done promote a firm and brings about referrals. The product of schools, quality or not, promote the school. The teachers are as good as their pupils meaning the successful teachers are those whose pupils performed excellently in the academics and moral standard. In short, brilliant, intelligent and well-behaved students promote the qualities of the teachers. Talents and skills discovered in youths, from the enabling environment created, in a nation could promote the nation into reckoning beyond what other areas of life could within a short period of time. The effective and efficiency of an institution promotes the institutions. Traditional praise-singers with the use of poetry, folklores, songs promote a stool, an exalted office of rulers, the stool, the cultures of the ethnics among several other gains. We have seen writers of repute that write to promote their people and race. Revered author, Chinua Achebe wrote about his race Igbo in all his popular works tracking the romance of the cultural values of the Igbos with those of their colonial masters. The retaining of one's ethnical names, wearing ethnic clothes, eating local ethnic foods, playing traditional sports, dancing to ethnic songs and dances, communicating in local dialects and showing confidence in the patronage of ethnic resources are forms of promoting the ethnic groups. I was glad to read online some years ago when a renowned publishing house advertised on publishing Nigerian writer books on all genres. This simply showed that the analytical findings of the researches most probably carried out by the firm confirmed that readers, who were their customers, were extremely interested to read about Nigeria's story from Nigerian authors' perspectives. By publishing Nigerian books, invitation and sponsoring Nigerians traditional singers and dancers abroad to perform in concerts and shows, permission for the displaying of visual artworks locally and abroad, exportation of local foods and drinks including herbs and what are locally produced are all forms of promotion of the national values (assets). On the flip side, the hard drugs pushers abroad are bad promoters (ambassadors) of the nation. Someone who carried the national passport and caught at airports by drug and human trafficking agencies and others for different illegal activities have promoted the nation in bad light. Everyone has a choice of the **promotion** for his personality, his family, his race, his faith, his affiliations and association, his alma mater and alumnus, his business network and institutions, the professional bodies such belongs, the political circle he pitches his tent among other ways of associations. With the huge social status on one's shoulder, no one would desire to be a promoter of illicit values, goods and services. How can a man born in a good family be engaging in cult-related activities? What about engaging in fraudulent jobs? Think of all the vicious acts that can ruin a reputation of self and those one shares one thing or the other with. Choices of promoting a brand or not is open to all. The working social infrastructures speak volume about a government. Landscapes, beautiful roundabouts, gardens and parks add values to the environment through the aesthetics not to talk of developed tourists sites promote a nation to the world. Many a nation recognized by UNESCO is as a result of consistent promotion of the resort places showing the wonders of creation. Performance of an administration promote the manifestoes of the party and personality of those at the helms of affairs to the nationals, within and in diaspora, and outside the shores. When a government, a party, an institution is celebrated, then such has gained a good brand status from the level of high reverence in the comity of nations vice versa. The style of adopted trademark and logo including the colours of a business promote the business. The moral precepts of an organization, religion, political, economic... promotes them. An interviewer could be sentimental or biased from the panel of panelists. If the interviewer intends to promote an ideology, such would not feature opposing sides to contribute. Each time I read articles inside prints or electronics, the featured names and the areas of interests, affiliations, ideology of the interviewee tell me what side of the coins the person would be. And the overall result is what exactly the writer or interviewer is promoting. Many authors of columns promote hatred against a system, a government, a nation, an institution, a faith, a culture when they fail to balance the equation. We can say we are all brands promoting one value or the other. Brands could take any form such as in personality of men and women, products and of services, norms, faiths, ideologies. The common thing that binds all activities of promotion and enhances promotion is the convinced state about the ideals, the norms, the quality, the distinct difference from others, what made the product or service thick in the market among peers, the generic functions, the viability of an idea, the tested and confirmed satisfaction derivable from consumption of a product or derives in patronage of a service or taking certain instruction.

An applicant has to promote what he has as qualifications from educational attainments in order to prove that he is the right peg (person) in the round hole (job). He did this through the original documents and the impressive performance in the course of interview. Sometimes, the way such applicant dressed to the venue may be additional promotion to win the vacant seat from other contestants attending the session. In the other way round, women who dress indecently indirectly have promoted indecency to the younger damsels who see them as models. The poser remains 'what do you promote with your mode of dress, the nicknames you bear, the uncultured manner you talk, the gang of people you move with or the company you keep? Is it the ideology you profess? Is it the religion you devout on? Is the ethnic you are originated from? Is it the dress ethic of the job? Is it to satisfy the lusts of your own body or personal desire? Is it to show self-ego? Is it to oppress or impress others? Whichever way, you are promoting your identity with all manners of behavior and attitudes.

Nations that protect her artefacts for visitors and observe the world tourism and cultural days understand how to promote the national values and assets. By the cultural days, everything about nations are promoted. Nationals wear native clothes, eat and promote the consumption of local foods and drinks, use traditional herbs, engage local artisans, promote the national festivals. In short, the nation is moving towards import-substitution and promoting the local industries to proliferate and expand.

Individual could promote his own brand provided such has certain natural endowments like literary work, artistic works, among other intellectual property. How would such promote his brand? Visit publishers of repute to produce your unpublished but scripted work. By promoting all the positive assets of inestimable values, individual is promoting thousands if not millions of others. Let me cite a simple illustration. If someone is asked about the inventor of an object, the name of the inventor, in the profile that would be read publicly, shall be related to his family, the schools he attended, the friends and colleagues, the nation such comes from and the tribe, his faith among several other data.

In retrospect, we promote things, persons, institutions, products, services, positions, status, ideology, faith, culture and limitless values to become a brand. Building a brand starts from the scratch. This is the reason we say that promotion started from the basics. Historians through revelation of rich histories could promote ethnic group and races. Testimonies about the generic values of a product and satisfaction derive from a service shall promote the products and services. Do you know that the faith-based institutions used to use concocted testimonies just to promote their worship places and faith to retain and increase the number of congregation? The already produced product or service is a brand-in-making. Every professional is born without the skills. It could be inherent where interests are created. Motivational speakers move from school to school to speak to children. Artistes perform on stages on streets before they started the film productions. Professional and successful sellers once knocked the doors on streets before becoming the international sellers with the use of technology today. All started to build their brands from the scratches.

A fellow thinker used to say 'people do not buy a book but the author. In some other climes, people buy book by its content and not the author. What would you say about a new author who has no prior credibility before such ventures into writing? Would a gifted writer be advised to abandon the innate trade? I object the notion. With my garnered experience and revelations of investigations, I know that all big oceans known today has a source from brooks; the credible author also started as unknown foetus. They created brands from the titles of their first works, by the colleges they attended, by the association they belonged to, by the faith they practiced, by other talents they exhibit, by the family they come from among others. I could recall that one of the workers of the companies that produced my first popular book demanded that I should pay for reviewers to write reviews about the work in order to attain credibility, I told him that the 'title' and the 'content' of the book were enough to sell the work and make it a bestseller within a very short period of time and the prophesy came to pass. A lot of ways can be used to promote a work. Column writings on the newspapers and magazine, local and international, could sell a message beyond the nooks and corners of a home, a town, a state and nations. Talk-shows on internet as online chats, interviews on television and radio about events, national resources could promote tourism of a nation to earn forex.

These are the categories of promoted things that must be continually promoted to make better impact in sales or effective demands, popularity and reliability in the marketplaces, offline and online:

a) **TANGIBLE GOODS**: These are consumable materials and the ones for the aesthetics referred to as accessories.

b) **VISIBLE SERVICES**: These are services that add values to the wellbeing of persons, places, events… as they add qualities to the items.

c) **INSITUTIONS** could be private and public-owned where goods and services are created for the public consumption

d) **EVENTS** varying from individual, organizations, government and non-governmental institutions

e) **NATURAL SITES** where tourists could visit as leisure. Such include the national parks, forest reserves among other ancient monuments

f) **POLICIES** which could be of individual, company, state, regional and nation. A type of ideology adopted by a nation or individual speaks volume about the nation or individual. In all sectors needed friendly policies that must be communicated by strong institutions and quality manpower.

g) **PROGRAMMES** that are presented towards making an event a reality and successful. People and institutions use handbills and media networks to promote what an event entails. Such must be communicated with the use of lucid words.

h) **IDEOLOGY:** This could be political, ethnic-based, institutional or religion ideology. Faithful must promote their ideology they profess by their manner and deeds. A devout Muslim is known from praying five times a day at due time. The morals of those who practice a religion must live by good examples. By so doing, they have promoted their faith to attract others. It is done by propagating house to house, office to office and institution to institution with handbills, stickers on moving vehicles and airtime on the media stations, parades along the streets, market places, parks and other public places.

i) **QUALITY OPERATING ENVIRONMENT:** it is done via the creation of enabling environment. Major in the latter is the availability of strong institutions and amended acts that would regulate and control the stakeholders activities towards making an environment conducive for operators of all forms of businesses- profit or not-for-profit based.

Generally, since evolution takes place, in persons, places, institutions, products, services, ideologies, every day as culture meets culture, compromises are done on the issue of ideology, there is need for alignments and realignments which must be communicated or promoted. Therefore, limitless are things to be promoted. Several symbols could be of relevance in such promotional activities depending on the target audience and the location of the people. Logo, trademarks, team jerseys, uniform dress, structures could define what a project stands for as a form of promotion. Just like the uniforms for pupils at public schools, the white uniforms of nurses, stethoscopes known with the medical professionals, the black over white shirt of the men of the bar and bench promote what professional leanings a person belongs to.

WHAT IS IN THE PROMOTING ITEMS?

"Limitless are resources and gains in items
Huge are the values seeking promotion
We promote what add values to living, simple"

Items are countless by our definition. All along, we have used several things to be promoted for individual, institution, government, and world at large. In nations are assets to be promoted like the flag, the currency, the resources, the successful nationals, the religion and ethnics with their values, the national sports and festivals, the coats of arms and the national heritage in tourist places. Within families are the brilliant children and wards who are exemplar in certain skills, those who are naturally endowed to invent machines and great artisanal objects among others that must be promoted as the pride of the families. In the nations are valuable non-human resources like lands, mineral resources, the institutions among the rest. Nation should collate all the information about them to sell the nation into the minds of the investors within and outside. In Nigeria, such carnivals like Calabar, Lagos and Argungun are promoted towards generating revenues and employments. The benefits from each of the items must be clearly defined and broadcasted for users. What should stop a political party that is of capitalist or socialist bloc to promote what they have in manifestoes to the people of the nation? One simple fact is clear to me as an author. Every good thing to a people and institution is the opposite to another. To the individual owner or institution, it is onus on each to promote, propagate what they have. The people they are focusing towards selling the messages or the ideas are like the customers in the marketplaces. The customers would make their choices based on interests they have for such hawked products or services. Promotion of all things within and outside shall propel the world into progress. They are presentable and highly valuable to meet the needs of the target users. Companies that are into manufacturing promote products that add values to life. The service providers present what would transform lives and property. Let us look at some other instances. Youths who are the leaders of tomorrow requires quality education and health services after the basic needs from the providers. Youths who have the brains and intelligence but from indigent home should promote self by mixing with the age group in school. From the sharing of ideas, they would learn how to acquire certificates without learning under any teacher in life. With the natural endowments on the youths, there is need to promote them to unveil the natural skills within them. Such is doable through exposure of the youths into seminars and workshops that are skills-based. In today's world, we have seen many professors who had never been to the four walls of classrooms receiving tutelage under any teacher. They were self-made literates. They were exposed to what they need to attain the dream height. They borrowed books for studying; paid for the external examinations and enrolled in online tutorials to make their papers and certificates.

In general, good, quality values and virtues are in the item, idea, product and service we promote for different category of people and institutions. The only determining factor of the success of a promotion is the kind of selected medium to do the promotion.

PROMOTION OF BRANDS

A brand is a product of an idea that is transformed into either a tangible product or visible services. The brand being promoted has no reference for not being an object or personality some years ago. No one who witnessed an event where citation about a successful person is being read would not dream of becoming a brand. The citation that is well composed and read in a lucid language has promoted the person. A brand person is a distinguished and celebrated person picked by consensus after several critical screening based on criteria in the midst of millions. Wake up from your slumber, discover the personality within you and strive to become a talk of the town. Distinguish yourself in your choice field of endeavor. It takes certain promotions that skyrocket a nothing to something. When something become a substance of value or of reference that is incomparable for a distinguished feature, then such has attained the status of a brand. A name can become a brand from the race or family such is birthed. A child born into affluence by affluent parents is already a brand in comparison with a child born to a wretched parent. Promotion has been the salt in the soup. Brands are all-encompassing. Everything that can be defined by special composition and distinguished characteristics is a brand. The word 'brand' is hidden attribute of people. Recall that precious stone like gold is always wrapped in the soil. It was when it is discovered and polished that it becomes valuable jewelry. Everyone is a brand like gold. Discover yourself and start image polishing to become a brand. A celebrated author was not born with pen in his hand. A professional and revered doctor was never in history born with stethoscope on his neck. All babies are born the same and tabula rasa but different natural endowments peculiar to the environment he's born and raised. Environment where they are born turn them into a brand. A child born with silver-spoon in his mouth does not know that his parents were rich before he was delivered as a baby vice versa. A prince does not know that his father is a king or from the royal family at birth. The environment turns him a brand.

<u>Being a brand from source does not mean that no promotion is needed</u>. Good product and service must be periodically branded to retain the loyal customers and gain new ones. Books from popular author need aggressive promotion from the serialization of the contents especially by the reviewers and analysts. Films

from award-winning thespians must be extensively promoted though the promotions of trusty, credible and bestseller authors and award-winning thespians may not consume much promotional efforts and money unlike the same products from novice in the industries. When a princess dresses, the princess in her distinguishes her from peers. When a child of the rich puts on a clothing and the peer group from the indigence home dress in a piece of cloth (stuff) that looks similar, the designer sellers would know the difference in maker, quality and price. It is not a matter of proud, one by innate is a promoter of what he wears, consumes, the class he belongs, the qualification he has attained among other outward disposition. Being a proud owner of a car does not mean 'pride'. It is promoting the natural endowment (God's favour) and grateful to the Almighty. In all the cases, as the noblest among us was reported to have said '**intention determines the action**'. No brand must be with pride in order to avoid ruin. Pride, they say, leads to a fall. In my clime where titles are worshipped, mention a name without the titles, the person would be frown at you. Call them to the podium with all the titles, they could spray you with mints of currency; you could win instant appointments and juicy contracts. In order to avoid digression, every brand is a title that lives with the owner for life.

Brands, from the last illustration, could be distinguished. You don't call an electrical engineer by medical doctor. An architect is different from an administrator unless such as moved further to obtain the educational certificate on the course of study at relevant institution. Every profession of a professional is a brand at source. The poser remains 'would the brand be the choice of the target clients?' This is the reason for promotion. A professor may lose his academic value if his contribution, from mere speech, in a discourse does not merit his status. Conversely, a student may be mistaken to be a professor with his apt and quality contributions in a public discourse. A reason for the award of the honourary degrees to people of creativity. Every profession is distinct even the local conventional artisans. Every aspirant to a public post has distinct features that would make them unique or different from one another. The position of individual media aides is to use attractive words to showcase what their bosses are made up of. Political parties in history won positions of authority on the leverage of their promotion of manifestoes and aspiring candidates. It is possible for parties to use propagandas to promote their political ideologies. We, by choice, can only distinguish all by value one profession than the other rendering the first so elevated and valuable to be a brand. Brand is inherent in all. It could be for personality, tangible product, visible services, ideologies and faiths. By their acts and attitudes popular known to be behaviours, personality is created, good or bad. On the two, popularity becomes the household name. A social miscreant is known with social nuisance to the society he finds himself. One can easily identify a drunkard by the irritating smell oozing out of his body and the staggering posture. A slut is identified at nights by the way she presents self to target prey through the lusts and showing of the cleavages without care.

Brands that would be promoted by analysts, marketers, advertisers, reviewers, promoters.. of items, institution, persons, objects, places… must have these:

a) **TITLE:** A person must have a baptismal or nickname name. My people in their wisdom, literally in English, say 'name of a child is his brake'. On the streets, every man is seen equal in status. The only distinguishing factor is the extra names from the family or linear status, marital, academics attainment, societal esteem or estimation among others. When a prefix like a title is attached before a name, the reverence is more intense. One can imagine the respect for Prince XXX or President YYY, the acceptability of a book written and addressed as Bestselling author of … or the award-winning… All the prefixes and suffixes of a name add more values to the status of the brands. Such later names or sub-titles could be for the promotion of an actor in a movie as a face of the movie. Tom and Jerry are popular brands for the cartoon stories. A good example is ***James bond*** being acted by different legends like ***Sean Connery, Roger Moore***. Such names, by meaning, spiritual or otherwise, would or could speak of the present, the past or look into the expectations in the future. Ascribing captivating, meaningful, decent and positive titles to an object, a town, an event, an institution would draw crowds. On individual, such person must be identified with a profession. Such should be living a socially responsible life especially married in nations and ethnics where marriage is a priority. Education level must be modestly high to enjoy being a revered brand. Sometimes, such must belong to a social club to enjoy being branded. Dreaming of a being a brand is working towards being valuable ambassadors to all the areas of connection to the family, tribe, schools, faith, businesses, association, community and the nation at large. For a business, the business name must be attractive to the public as it has become part of the society. Such name must not belittle the ethnic, the faith, the political system and others in the business environment where the business is a subset. In this case, the business owners that are dreaming to have brand name must not step on toes in the naming of the business. All the procedural steps must be taken to avoid being tagged fraudulent business. From the adverts on radio and television of a business, one would know the brands that are broadcast to fraud innocent clients and customers. The business must have corporate name registered with the corporate affairs commission or the ministry of commerce and industry with all documents required submitted, critically examined and endorsed. Social institutions and organizations must have a **trademark** like the corporate firms. The location of such business which may boost the acceptability must not be omitted. The graphic writing, the business logo, the trademark and others for the business must be properly done to promote the business at outset. The profiles and attainments of the team of directors submitted to the corporate affairs commission for registering should be ones that would promote the business. The next in line is to consider the letterhead and all materials that would carry the business names and the logos including other saleable information to the target customers or clients all in a way to promote the business from outset. The selection of titles for the products from the company should be one that would elevate the status of the business. Use wrong titles and you lose your potential patronage and sales. Products must register with a unique and attractive name with the right regulatory authority to ensure promotion is done.

The use of business ethics such as the wearing of customized uniforms by staff members and the executives from homes to offices could be another way of promoting a business. In all the offices and homes should be supplies of the products. Competition must be available with a name. Name in short is a brake and a control. Towns must have names that would be attractive to outsiders and listeners. It should be re-named if such name attract some evils. Just like in a name that must be after bad models, animals, beast and related, we must name the towns, the streets, the nation by devilish or cursed names in order to have positive promotion of the town, nation and the attractions within. A town named after popular role models are attractive to tourist and investors. All the aborigine son and daughters of the soil shall be proud to be from the town. No one likes to be known with miscreants and dictators. Every product must have captivating name called title. Do you know that the name of a school could serve as turn-on and turn-off for the prospective clients? A publicity secretary was on air to promote the party manifestoes of his party. To my assessment, he failed woefully. To a layman, his defence would be accepted hook, line and sinker. What were his propositions? "Our cardinal programme is in the acronym 'HEAPS' meaning Health for all, Empowerment, Agriculture, Poverty alleviation and Social justice. Why did I score him low? He failed to inform the public on the census of those people and institutions that the agenda shall focus to work upon. If I were the publicity secretary, with the consent and support of the party, we shall work upon generating the population of all institutions and people by their bio data across the state we are intending to govern. With the census, we shall collate what each institution lack and what could be added to add greater values, the number of people and the jobs including the amount they earn hence we can determine the disposable income and living cost. With all these in places and how we would generate revenues to sustain all the projects within the time limits for each, the hearts of the target electorates have been won for the election already. Such title of goods and of services must be easy to pronounce by all Toms, Dicks and Harry. Sometimes, a title of a tangible product or service may need to have sub-titles to catch the interests of the prospective customers and publicists, young and old, no matter the gender, faith, ideology, ethnic, qualifications and affiliations.

At early stage of my life, I like such film series under the titles 'The Invincible man' the Incredible Hulk', The man from Atlantic ocean'. 'The Ruppies', 'The Charlies angels', 'The fantastic four' among several others. Actors like **Bruce lee** and **Jackie Chan** would remain evergreen in memory of people and marketers. One quick reference is that both are connected to a nation, China. They are good brands and worthy entertainment ambassadors promoting the Chinese culture with their martial art produced in films. The art is being sold to the world is another sample of promotion to generate forex for the People's Republic of China. The duo are like the **Damendra Amita bachar, Shashikapur** of India entertainment industry. To both, they are household names in acting just as several others are brands under different professional leanings. America would forever extol the virtues of **Roger Moore** and the rest actors acting James Bond. Say Steve Jobs of Apple incorporation and the whole world bow for the American brand in the digital revolution industry. All these are ambassadors and brands to their nations. I believe the sub-titles (explicit, motivational, practicable towards being my own boss') of my first book "***Jobs with zero capital***" further add values to the major title. In the title are references to some other supplementary books and references. The latter books are indirectly promoted to capture the minds of the buyers. Publishers used to have list of books from the same author or the same company at a page in a book to create pre-sale awareness. The accolades like 'author of the bestselling...' by the publishers while introducing the author and the title is a way of promotion. When a company writes 'since 1890', what does it mean? It is passing a message to the customers and prospective ones that the brand is a trusted and has being a trustworthy brand for over a century. Is this not a way to promote a brand?

Generally, it is not just the captivating title and the supporting sub-titles of a product or service that promote a product or service but all things like the nation, the race, the association, the business name, the revered public figures that endorse the item, the ethno-religion endorsement among others.

b) **TITLE MUST BE CONSPICOUSOLY WRITTEN FOR SHORT AND LONG SIGHTED POTENTIAL CUSTOMERS**. Products and services must have a name that would be attractive to the ears of the target clients or patrons. We have names just as everything has a name. We must be proud to bear and answer to our titles called names. The topic of my first book gave the book the popularity it instantly enjoyed in the book market. I confidently told my publisher's representative who demanded for more money for promotion that the title and the content unambiguously presented would capture the minds of the readers and buyers. Names could spur to productive or otherwise if bad and offensive names are used. Bad name repel potential admirers to join a party or to vote an aspirant. The wrong use of words as sub-titles may be the obstacle to get results. For a product to be packaged for customers, a title that does not look bold enough may not attract long distance customers who could have interests in procurement. A business that is established very far away from the road must have big signpost depicting the nature of business and the purpose of existence. Bold fonts for the good names (titles) shall add values to the promotional instinct of the managers or the management team. Manifestoes of a party in a multi ethnic and multi religion must respect all the two determining factors to success. Translate them into different languages of the dialects and at least the major tribes in the nation.

c) **THE SUB-TITLES**: In many cases, the sub-titles speak volumes about the title. It could be one that would explain concisely what the title stands for in meanings. I believe the sub-titles of my books used to work magic turning them into **highest rated** books (Ref: amusa abdulateef books on kobobooks.com). It is onus on the author, producer of films, song writers, poet writers, playwright, the makers of consumable brands and service providers to use a combination of attractive titles and sub-titles. Many education service business owners either loss or gain patronage simply because of the names or titles for the establishment. Titles promote the goods and the services.

d) **SYNOPSES**: Every buyer of a product is apparently impatient at markets, online and offline. The use of concise synopses used to capture the mood and emotion of the prospective buyers or clients. It is suffice for the use of independent and experienced preview writers. When a book enjoys right synopsis, the book has been promoted to the customers across the nations.

e) **APT PRESS RELEASE**: I endorsed the press release of my first work as it really spelt out my reasons for researching and writing the book. It was what I was thinking. What are we dragging at? All the people in charge of promotion of the goods and services must be those who really have perfect understanding of the vision, mission, objectives, ideas, values.. that must be promoted. Beating about the bush is a wrong way of promotion.

f) **PACKAGE OR OUTWARD DISPOSITIONS:** When I decided to release some digital books on internet, I chose to use cover pages with no import of pictures and graphics. The letterings, the fonts, the background colouring and some other features from the combination of Microsoft word and corel draw produced unique cover pages that are very attractive. For a business-conscious person, the outlook of a thing really matter to promote what one has in mind. A leader should work on road networks and their beautification with road signs, flowers, trees, streetlights, gardens and parks among others to promote the aesthetic environments to the visiting foreigners among whom could be investors. An untidy home is uninviting to a visitor to a family. Good books that serialized the contents of scriptures of a faith shall promote the religion to others from other faiths outside the faith. A school and all institutions that are not tidy and properly organized may lose value and at the brink of collapse. For a consumable product, graphic designs of the wrap covers of a products always create good buying impression especially for docile buyers. Such buyers see such attractive cover or wrapper as a sign of quality of the content. A service station that is well packaged attract clients.

g) **INWARD COMPONENTS OR THE CONTENT:** By this, the three t's namely trustworthy, transparency and truthfulness are the keys to huge promotion to ensure patronage. Leaders at the helms desire visitors from other nations to pay business visits and probably establish bilateral business ties with the nation and the business stakeholders within; such must have done huge work to create ever enabling business environment. Of products and services, the best way to promote such brand is through the content which must provide the generic function. This is being honest with the target consumers and not otherwise. When a baby is given honey, he would not ask for anything outside for the sweet taste. An ethnic should attract attentions with right cultural values. No race and nation shall have its tourism developed with poor attractions. Give the target patrons and matrons what would serve as the baits and you enjoy unanticipated patronage. No matter the benefits derivable by the tourist, business and non-business, none would ever risk his dear life to a place where there is insecurity. You have promoted what you have with simple provision of aesthetics in the environment. Brace up to promote your nation, your political party, your ethnic group, your religion, your community, your business, your educational institution, your alma mater, your social clubs, your places of interests among others with good inward and outward disposition. Ensure you walk the talk always!

h) **THE ACTORS THAT WOULD PROMOTE THE BRAND:** The publicist is a factor in the promotion of items and values. There are simple mistakes by the makers and sellers that could be avoided (Ref: 'winning huge sales and increasing clients' base'). Sometimes, external models are recruited to promote certain item. For a tourist from abroad, there must be communicators that must be hired by the nation. A company needs language translators or some multi-linguist to serve the role of the publicists. The choice of the presenters and promoters of an item in idea, philosophy, a product or service makes a brand an acceptable brand. Many times, celebrated professionals and the retired technocrats are the right people to promote a brand. It is like an endorsement of the brand.

i) **THE CHOICE INSTITUTIONS THAT WOULD ACT OR DISPLAY THE PROMOTION**: Promotion of brands must select the institutions that are appropriate for the job. School kits and educational materials are best promoted to the school proprietors, the stakeholders in the education sector within and outside. From the earlier illustrated example in 'e', there are specialized institutions that must be involved to promote certain specialized values. It took a political party in Nigeria recently to package the party into victory in a general election. There are brand makers for politicians. Nations could afford to employ the services of the renowned specialized publicists and promoters for different projects to be promoted. Many natural resources lying idle in a nation need those who can present them to the right institutions in the world.

j) **THE TIME OF PROMOTION:** Time is a factor that determines success and failure. Everyone must target the right time that would play positive role in the success of what is intended to be promoted. Chilling drinks are promoted when the temperature is hot vice versa. Thick cloths are promoted a short time to rainy and cold seasons. Many a brand may not be popular to prospective customers if they are advertised to the public at the wrong time. The media has the knowledge on when a brand should be placed to attract the highest crowd that may follow it and probably make purchase. The last quarter of the year used to be peak sales period in western nations by studies.

k) **THE MEDIUM THAT WOULD BRING THE BEST RESULTS:** By the word 'best results', we mean the ever-growing unprecedented gains for the establishments or sales in terms of profits for the profits-focused institutions. Politicians could use different modes to promote what they have in the cooler for the people. They could take the style of products marketers moving public place to public places with the most vocal as the team leaders. Jingles and live drama could be staged at different places and electronic media houses to announce what they have in stock for the electorates at different times including how they plan to achieve the objectives. Nations always use the office of the minister or Secretary of information to launder the image of the government. Some used to have certain institutions that must shoulder the responsibilities of promoting the good virtues of the leaders. Many called them propagandists even when they are broadcasting correct messages about the government. What is expected of running a business, political, national, professional leaning and faith-based in jingles that are free from filths, hate speech and acts, abuses and sentiments in media stations that have won different awards especially as the widest network, or the most viewed station, or the most listening to among the stations, the most popular of the media brands across continents? Of course, such stations by the recognitions through the awards would attract the best of minds and potential tourists, investors, customers or referrals for the items being promoted including the products or services of business-based institutions. With this guarantee, the business owners smile to banks; the party won landslide election; the tourist places got increased patronage and the hospitality business and the value chains get instant improvement; the nation is more known to millions from the publicity and there is possible value exchanges and respect for one another from the value sharing. It is a gross mistake and miscalculation to place adverts about any item especially of the products or of the services at stations or selected print media that does not have the reach and popularity- local, regional, national and international. If a station that is about to commence operation meant business, it should start skeletal service free of charges test-running the engines and some popular on-air-presenters probably from the reigning stations. I gave out free e-book at outset of promoting my e-book selling site. Nations could promote the tourism sector through visa free programme. Nations could attract investors to the nation through tax-free and duty-free on all machines being imported for the business. Agri-business could be promoted with the free inputs like land, tractors, storage facilities and high yield seeds. Through this, the concept and the contents that make the programme would have been promoted. In the case of the programming of stations, constant announcements with attractive jingles with creative attractive words must be employed to get fans and friends of the programme and the stations glue to their radio or television. Styles of presentations of the announcers would play a great role in the attractions of audience to the show. Efforts must be made before business operation commence to edit every concept and content that could repel target people and institution before such is eventually aired. Field research should be done to be aware of the styles in vogue which the target listeners and viewers would key into.

l) **ORIGIN OF THE BRAND:** A nation that has promoted its tourism sector and the people to outside world would fear less about failing in the market. It should not be forgotten that the brilliant intellectual property and rich history including historical festivals are part and parcel of tourism. Everyone likes to associate with nations of popular figures, warriors of repute, big industrialists, influential kings and queens aside all the attraction places. People buy books from Nigerian author as a result of the brands the names of the Chinua Achebes, Wole Soyinkas, Chimamandas, Ahmed Yerimas of this world had made for the nation to become a brand in the intellectual world. The names of social activists like Tai Solarin, the Kuti family, Awolowo, Sardauna, Azikwe among others are enough to sell Nigeria as a brand to other parts of the world. This is the reason for having punitive measures for those nationals that are soaking the nation's name in the dirty waters outside the shores through criminalities like drug trafficking, armed robbery and the likes in vicious acts that are punishable by laws across the nations. Most institutions, nations, associations, professional bodies and customers dream of patronizing or consuming what are produced from other nations that are of good brands by promotions. Consuming such would serve as if they are living in the nation as citizens. Every imported item, policy, equipment to produce goods or run a service must have the right address of importing nation such as 'Made in ...'. Or the engravement of the popular company that manufactured or processed such good in order to attract target sales in the global market. Suffice a reason why nations work on the good brand of their nations through consistent positive promotions. They disown such makers from their nation that produce inferior goods that may tarnish the good image of the nation. Customers used to ask about the designers of what fellow customers wear.

UNHEALTHY PROMOTION AND BRANDS

Much has been said about the advantage of promotion of products and services in particular. Despite the fact that promotions of the policies and national values may have increased the number of possible patronage, there is the need to look at the other sides of the coin. It has been a disadvantage to several businesses to be viable in the wake of unhealthy promotion of brands of products and services. In Nigeria recently, the telcos are threatening to withdraw their services and related institutions as a result of dwindling sales. In the nation, the network providers are engaging in slashing the prices massively. An airtime credit of 100 may enjoy 400 worth of credits while a purchase of 1000 data may enjoy 4000 data and the unhealthy promotion has never stopped. There is the need for the regulatory institutions to stop all forms of price promotions to outwit one another to the improvement of the quality of services alone. When the quality of service remains what is used to promote the information and communication business, then the unsettled subscribers may not search for lower prices and freebies but stay with choice quality of service.

Many companies today have closed shops and thereby sent thousands to the labour markets as unemployed. In Nigeria, there were nine network providers that were licensed to operate. By 2017, only three are surviving while another is struggling as a result of soaring debts despite the popularity as the network was said to have over 20 million subscribers. Five providers had become a story. The evils of price cut promotion and other ways of giving out discounts are leading to drop in patronage for some brands. These cause confusions to the customers. Government could arrest the closure of businesses by halting all forms of price and discount promotion but compete in quality which the customers should decide themselves. This should be done to save jobs.

1.3 METHODS OF PROMOTION: HOW DO WE PROMOTE?

> *"Apply right aesthetics*
> *Adopt and act good virtues*
> *Be conscious of your tastes*
> *Speak positive things about your nation and institutions*
> *And by these, you've promoted the brands"*

We promote by living by example. We promote good virtues by being exemplary model and engage in mentoring others. Many a religion priest and teacher fail to have followers living the precepts and true teachings of their faiths simply because they do not walk the talk. Leave Starting from nations; they have a lot of things to promote the nation towards attracting investors and great brains. Such could be the style of urban plan and social infrastructures availability at the right places. A nation that deals or convert the slum into highbrow areas with working infrastructures, security at all places with all the gadgets fitting at appropriate places, proto-type houses with flags and well painted in unique uniform colours, aesthetics and clean environment, discipline citizens, fast bureaucracy, free visa policy for certain professionals, tax free on certain aspects in all sectors towards creating enabling business environment, strong institutions among others; people and business interests shall be attracted. On institutions, they could replicate all the stated points under the attractions anticipated from the nation to promote the nation. Product makers should be proud of their products at any gathering. It is a thing of pride for one to speak volume of a good product or a quality service by action and talks. Nation should be proud of her celebrated achievers in all facets of life such as the renowned academics, the great philosophers, renowned institutions, the popular festivals, the rich histories, reputed authors, the honest and truthful leaders in politics, the main tourist places and the national values among others have different ways to promote them into greater limelight. We see all these as either products or services. And the institutions, individuals, places, events to be the promoter are the producers or service providers. One can boast of a good product likewise an effective service. This is a reason why producers and service providers must invite criticism from professionals before public display. We promote by what we do, say and act with all the natural and available resources at our beck and call. Government could send emissaries and ambassadors to sensitize the other nations over the stated items worthy of promotion earlier. This depends on the level of dynamism, intelligence, exposure, experience, creativity, courage, confidence and ingenuity. Retreat, workshops, seminars, road shows, exhibitions, symposia, public address through paid-publicists or the likes, special documentary could be used to publicize a product, service, company, nation, position or anything we call a brand. Sometimes, tours can be used to herald the coming of a product or service to the market. Many cars enter into auto-mart after several months of promotion. The same is applicable to intellectual property like books, films, songs among others. Months before live concert of popular singers, promotion would be massive and intense just as football match between titans as in el-Classico in Spanish La Liga match between rivals Real Madrid and FC Barcelona. Such **promotion** may include series of pre-show interviews, road shows for publicity, featuring popular figures in other areas of life as partners. Some used to have partners from other credible institutions. Tickets are always sold out months before the kick-off. Free samples of the product to people at different places is also a good way to promote goods and services. Test-running of media station, auto product in strategic places add values to the popularity strength of a product before emergence at the public place for patronage. In the issue of book selling, many retailers adopt dynamic selling strategies to attract buyers. Some of these are 'search inside' by the likes of amazon.com, google.com and barnes and noble.com. Freebies at trade fairs connect potential patrons to a product and service. I have witnessed trade fairs where banks opened bank accounts for customers free of charge. Zero-account attracted millions of banks customers to open accounts with a popular bank that has won local and international awards for years in Nigeria. Campus to campus shows, markets to markets road shows have popularized many products and services. Pre-meeting, pre-show where enlightenments on the reasons why a product or service is needed by people, and all others done before promote all. Brands must be promoted in unique and dynamic ways before the formal introductions. Use aesthetics for different stages of production. During the period, the big guns in the society meet to announce the product and service to the world. Writers who are specialized on different courses and professions do these through their pens in black and white. Formal presentation of goods and visible services through different means serve good way to announce the package to the world markets. Interviews done prior to the public launches are parts of the methods of unveiling the products and services at outset. Singers used to use different nicknames to sell (promote or hype) their brands. In Nigeria, we have different prefixes in names such as 'General' 'President', 'Commander' and 'Admiral'. Through the style of dressing and the language of the artistes, the nationality and the ethnic of origin are known to the public. In public and private concerts or at social parties, they can praise-sing a product or service to boost the image of such in the market just as Sikiru Ayinde Barrister; the prefix 'barrister' is a brand used to promote the real baptismal name of the artiste; the late Fuji musician, regarded to as the originator of the kind of music, from Nigeria did for Disney World in Florida, America. People can use their pens and natural intelligence to push a product or service to the throats and belly of customers or clients. One of the attributes of the promoters using pen, mouth and other choice parts of the body or tools is that they have dynamic and creative ways to present their facts together. When a product is being earmarked for production, there is the need for prior creation of awareness. The sales and marketing department must brainstorm on the mode of **promotion** and where it must start, the editorial crew for books and newspapers must work on the titles of the piece, the titles and compositions to propagate the contents, the content writers and managers of radio and television programmes must develop concepts that would attract people and create traffics across the length and breadth of the nations.

Those assigned with the responsibilities illustrated above must be moving with the trends in the business environments where customers or clients are targeted. Many questions must come to mind. Such includes 'what is the best way to pass the message? What is the language they understand most? What about the medium they can be mostly relevant in the dissemination of the contents or conceptual idea?

In view of the above, I could recall how we work on a project. All the stakeholders put head together over how we could reach all corners of the world. Our consensus agreement that **promotion** is the key to attract traffics of likely clients or customers. But, there must be prioritized methods of reaching out to target people, identified places and prioritized institutions. I know of schools that are located at strategic places where companies used to come to customize through partnership. Many proprietors are aware that the company are promoting their content through the partnership with them. Many of the beverage companies gave the pupils their products free to the staff and students in order to win their desire for the products and serve as free publicists outside the school premises.

We have witnessed companies that sponsored subjects-based competitions in order to promote what the institution stands for. Some are into promoting sports especially football contests and leagues. By so doing, both partners would have international popularity. Let me cite some popular samples of partnership. Real Madrid Football club is popular through the stars the club used to buy for the team. Many of the stars pull crowds from all continents to increase the clubs' revenue generation ability from the sales of kits, endorsements, souvenirs sales, players loaning and selling transaction with favourable buy-out clauses, promotion of companies' products and services for charges. Barcelona Football Club and Arsenal once partnered with emirate airline. The clubs are in Europe popularizing an aviation firm based in United Arab Emirates. Nations have made efforts to register their nations in the world map through bidding to host international competitions. Many relatively unknown nations in soccer business are injecting billions of dollars towards making the nations and their potentials known to the whole world. Many in hospitality business host fashion and design shows, awards nights, music shows, film premiere, launching, symposia... simply to create awareness to the facilities at the institutions for clients.

Let me use my personal experience in the publishing sector to explain the importance of selecting the right **promotion** for all that we intend to promote to catch attention. From the word go just like any other professionals, I had been thinking about how to promote my brand in writing and publishing of my research-based books. Then, I initially decided to write in a unique way after studying the styles of writing of the internationally renowned authors whose books have lived on international sites for decades even after their deaths. I got some books of the living legends in authoring of books especially the bestsellers. Sincerely, at outset, the book "How to make friends and influence more people" by the renowned author **Dale Carneggie** which I read while in the youths service place of assignment really did the magic. Some further steps were added to the style I chose or the path I took to establish myself in the literary industry. Such include the use of motivating words in phrases and sentences, capitalizing or 'bold' of certain emphatic words. Sometimes, underlining and italic of such word or words would pass the message. When someone asked me how my first book was so popular in the market. I told him that there are several factors. A writer could use attractive pseudonym or co-author with someone who is already a brand in the writing industry to sell and promote his own brand as a form of announcing his intellectual worth to the book environment. Today, there are collaboration works from the song artistes. Upcoming thespians are being introduced among the arrays of stars in films to promote the newly discovered talents. Others features for book promotion are:

a) **THE TITLE OF THE BOOK:** At the outset, I thought of such title that would pass the message or content as a-must-read for buyers. A list of titles were listed. Out of the lists, I chose the most captivating that would catch attention of all even a lay man on the streets. At this juncture, I ask: "what is the title of your business? What is the title of your service? What is the title and sub-titles of your corporation? What do you name your institution? Does your title look simple to interpret attract general public?

b) **THE BRAND OF THE PUBLISHERS:** I carefully investigated and consulted widely about getting facts about the reach of the publishers and their working partners. In fact, consideration of different publishing houses across United States and United Kingdom was done. I read widely and shared my mind with different minds before selecting one. I was attracted mostly by the partners the companies are working with. The partner is one that is reputable in the publishing industries with tentacles across the nations even in Africa. Working or establishing partnership with a brand is like a man that befriends and used to stay at a perfume seller shop. Such would be smelling nice like the seller. Every right thinking person would like to be working with the affluent and the brilliant minds. In this case, "what is the actual brand you are promoting or intend to join as partner? What type of brand in a sector you identify with? Which brand in institution or partner are you interested to work with?

c) **PUBLISHER'S BASE AND CONNECTION NETWORK:** I considered the book reading environment. By this, I mean an environment where its people have a very high reading culture. No author would not appreciate such environment to have crowds of lovers of his intellectual property and earning royalty. Do you look into or consider the coverage of the partners and institutions you are working with in order to have right amount of promotion? If a business is in partner with a business that has its reach across the nations, then such has also wear international brand. Publishing my works with international publishers that have all it takes to reach the world within a short term has made me an internationally recognized author. What I cannot, and may never, achieve with the resources at my fingertip is enjoyed through working with renowned participant in the publishing sector. Many song artistes release their singles online to attract the international records label that would sign them on. Is this not a good path to promote one's ideas, values, assets and resources?

d) **THE COMPILE INFORMATION ABOUT THE PROMOTIONAL STRATEGIES:** A critical look into the series of promotion entices me into working with the publisher. Imagine a publisher that has television house, connection to over 500 media outlets, over 25,000 retailers among which are the largest retailers or market places. Watch out for the wide reach of the partners or the institutions you are about to work with. I visited radio stations to have first-hand information about where such reach and the quality of the listeners across the nations. I always do the same for the print media to be informed about the ones that would give me the best service in the promotion of my works. Is this not a right step?

e) **THE PARTNERS IN BUSINESS:** The companies that partnered with the publishers attracted yours sincerely to choose the publishing firm. A publisher that has over 60,000 published books and a broadcasting media as one of the sister company; what are the other platforms to enhance popularity of your item? Many of which are bestsellers and converted to blockbuster films. Have you considered the past and recent achievements of the partners in mind as done by me? The enviable track records have promoted the partners at sight for consideration. What you lack, others have. A brand you dream to become is available within you just by the click of a few buttons of computer connected to internet!

The above steps should be taken by others producing or selling other products outside print-based business. Work with partners that have good brand. Develop interest in knowing the partners before you engage the selected. Choose right name that would not attack or degrade 'the most sensitive' ethno-religion values. Climb up the ladder to attain a brand status through public endorsements by the popular figures in all facets of life. Feel free to chat and discuss about your product and service at chat rooms, online conversation, public discourse, premiere your film at popular cinema and art gallery at the right time when your invitations shall be honoured hence you enjoy a full house. Use press to promote your goods and services. Have press briefings. Parley with journalists and broadcasters. Work with celebrated thespians, artistes, artists and popular figures in all institutions close to you to popularize your products and services. Never use negative characters to avoid relegating the popularity of your items. Be nice always. Commission the goods at the right markets. Imagine unveil reading the excerpts of your books at the hall of a school. For promotion of different items being spoken of from different people, places and institutions, there are peculiar methods of promotion to achieve set objectives. Besides, there are several promotional plans that are in place to boost the popularity of all kinds of works and items. On printed works like the promotion of books is an all-inclusive project as it involves the authors, the librarians online and offline, the publishers and the independent sellers like the retailers and the distributors. I was not surprised the use of international market places like amazon.com, barnes and noble.com, rakuten.com, kobobooks.com, alibris.com… and the use of popular search engines like google.com, ask.com, and the social media handles that are available to retailers in different corners of the continents. It shows that there is a viable business working relationship between the publisher and those mentioned. All of them are internationally recognized brands that started gradually but consistently. I believe that a book that is published and promoted by brand publisher shall in no time become a bestseller too. Brands promote brands to become bigger brands. A book co-authored by renowned two credible authors would become a bigger brand among books. A film co-produced by award winning producers shall become an instant hit blockbuster in the markets. An aspirant that is nominated for a post by credible party and politicians of reputable character shall easily win the attention of the voters and eventually win the votes. If a renowned independent marketers pick up interest in the marketing and selling of a product, such product would become a household name within a short period of time. To become a household name, one must be ready to make sacrifices. After the developing of my site got to the peak, we discussed about what we can do to promote the site. Several ways were suggested. At outset, by consensus, we accepted the use of freebies where free downloads of a book is done and another is placed at a small price for the visitors who can afford the amount. Of course, first timers would like to have a taste or sampling of the job to be upload for sale. The only condition based on the security code in the site was that the person who enjoyed the free download can only do so after dropping his or her email address where the free e-book shall be dropped by automation. I believe that I would become a better brand with the contract with a global brand in the publishers. Working has provided room for the author to become an international brand from a mere local brand. I discovered many other ways to promote my intellectual property through reading of print materials. I came across how one can promote the materials through special blogs for the actual product. I got message about **adsense** of google, how I can promote the materials cum books as an affiliate of some established companies who have the reach faster internet connection and network. In fact, it is confirmed that many who give out service as freebies, especially the social media entrepreneurs, do so to attract traffics from all over the world. And later, sell advertisements estimated by the classes of people and the reach of the product or service owners.

Factually, every tangible good, with huge popularity as a partner, is a promoter of others. Thinking about how to hit it from my works, I chose to partner with institutions that are good brands. I wrote proposals to tertiary institutions under partnership agreement on how both brands could hit the online market with international book business environment.

Generally, to achieve the anticipated optimum result on all forms of selected strategy of **promotion**, the following steps are relevance:

a) The words to be communicated about the brand must be critically analyzed after properly scripted for proper editing, screening and properly filtered as no intending customer would allow a message that would downgrade their ethno-religion beliefs, national values, ideologies, personalities and social affiliations.

b) Editing of the contents must be given to a third party who are experts on the fields and not the writers of the promotional words. In most cases, content managers are needed to prepare the promotion jingles for writing, editing, vetting and producing. I edited the cover page of the first book published with the international POD publisher and also endorsed the press release before it was released to over five hundred media houses.

c) Researching into those medium of promoting the contents based on the popularity and the wide reach. As we have suggested and recommended to the political parties and their aspirants including the nations, there must be deep research on what to promote as adequate information about the media stations, electronic media and other means of promotion must be sought before going public.

d) Pay for aggressive promotion time. Be consistent in the promotion. Never create vacuum. When a listener to radio used to hear about a product on a popular programme on a popular radio, the audience following the station and the programme are possible buyers of the produced or service being constantly announced to their ears. The same also applies to the television and digital stations. Nations that seek huge revenues from tourism must invest heavily on the promotion on all other brands that would add values to the tourist places. Such includes the traditional sports, ethnical values, popular festivals and popular towns by historical perspectives and those of personalities across all professional fields of life among others.

e) Promotion jingles, write-ups, articles, presentation papers, interviews must be cultured and free from abusive words. Many a product or service flops in the market from the hostilities created at the time of promotion. A good product that is actually target at a particular user must be friendly to all non-users because the field studies have confirmed to the fact that the buyers of a product or patronage of a service does not necessarily mean that he is the user. Such may intend to buy, as the breadwinner, for the dependents at home, offices or service stations. Sometimes, they could be independent shoppers or paid shoppers shouldered with responsibility of shopping for list number of people in internal displaced persons camps, staff members in a company or conglomerate, public or private institutions and places. If hiding or disguising about a brand would sell the product or service, please hide or change the titles found irritating. Many use pseudonyms instead of their real names to make positive impacts in the market. Many co-produce a work in order to enjoy the popularity of the popular persons to announce his own entrance into the market. If the need for short drama. Comics, animation, comedy… would add instant values to the promotion, engage in the step.

f) One should promote goods and services when staff members are mandated to wear customized dress of the company. National values could be promoted with hoisting of the national flags at all structures, in the offices of institutions, coat of arms on the clothes, using the national products, wearing national clothes or ethnical dresses on by the people.

In marketing and selling parlance, the pre-sale promotion like using the words like **'coming soon'**, **releases soon**, or 'out on so so date' would prepare the minds of the prospective buyers and bulk distributors including the retailers ready to be among the sellers. Announcing a product or service months before the official launching or opening of the business shall create huge public awareness ahead. In the high book reading environment, 'coming soon' books used to be booked ahead just like football contests, boxing contest, film premiere, popular entertainment show, and the rest where the tickets are sold out before the d-day. It is right for a new business to start with smallest sizes of variants. Books should be promoted with e-book first. When the content is well accepted, the paperback and hardcover should enter the market.

Many a business use lottery, sponsored competitions and contests, freebies, free tickets, free seminars, free samples, free services among others to promote their products and services to the target customers. A nation could assemble all her talented artistes in song and drama including the books from authors within and organize festivals of intellectual property to outside world. This promotion of the talents and products from the identified talents would be a major source of forex and employment generation. In Nigeria that is multi-ethnic and multi-religions, it is easy to collate huge number of talents from different fields for branding and rebranding as national assets and values (products and services) for selling to the worlds to earn forex and boost local industries. Individual artistes especially among the singers, poets and the writers could have creative villages for users from within and outside. The thespians could have film village where all their scripting, rehearsals, acting and productions are done. Nations could brand the industry with the finance of the public film villages, visual artistes' centres and writing academies to enhance (promote) the arts. However, some costly mistakes are made by some in the course of promoting them. We have detailed these while explaining the 'simple mistakes of promotion' in the book "**Winning huge sales and increasing clients' base**" by the same author)

Other ways a firm introduces the product or service of the company to the public is through creation of suspense inside the full-page of newspapers and monologue on the electronic media ending with '**watch out**' or **coming soon**'.

BRAINS BEHIND QUALITY PROMOTION

Having established the inevitability of promotion to develop self or personality, business, institution, nation and the world at large, we must look into the versatile drummers behind the scene of the captivating dancing steps. These are producers of the contents. Let me start with an illustration of a popular on-air-personality whose concepts are always fascinating. The credible and seasoned broadcasting man relocated to another media station probably to seek green pasture. The performance of his productions, in comparison to the first station, was below expectation. It was not the concept that was bad but the producer was not of quality. In nations, ministers fail in their official roles because they are bad promoters as leaders of their respective ministries. They lack vision and mission on how to promote different policies under their ministries. The promoters must be:

a) Highly dynamic in creativity. He should use what is in vogue that attracts positive developments and could add values to life.

b) Highly social and socially connected with different people to be aware of what can persuade or dissuade them into patronizing

c) Have full understanding of the brands being promoted and must at all times be ready to engage all on the brands. He or she must be able to talk widely on the concepts that must be promoted.

d) Must be someone that can introduce initiatives and innovations at any point in time. The introduction of the use of social media handles like instagram, facebook live and others has promoted the radio to become partly television as listeners that tuned to the pages of the social media handles could see live broadcast from the radio stations.

e) Compare notes with some background personal staff. Good athletes used to have special trainers that are paid from their purse. The likes of the Portuguese football talent, Cristiana Ronaldos of this world always come to mind. As a promoter or producer, have some people that are producing you. These people work behind the scene to bring about perfect or near-perfect job. Never rely on your instincts, personal wisdom or brilliance and intelligence alone. The wise is he who learns from other people's wisdom. Be a pupil to others even though you are the most revered in your place of work. I used to read the editorial reports of different newspapers in order to read between the lines from the opposing views and standpoints to issues. By this, one gets the necessary balance in later presentations.

f) Must be able to promote at the right time when crowd-pulling programmes are on especially the call-in programmes. I mean, placing the advert during live programme that have rooms for social interaction between the listener and viewer from the comfort of their homes and offices.

g) Be critics of his chosen words and other items for promotion. Be self-critics before you broadcast the message. Review the works before you air it. Repackage the contents from the studio of the owners before you promote. Always be conscious of the censor boards regulating the activities of a producer as a promoter. Never indulge in promoting illicit items that would be dangerous to living and hazardous to the environment as pollution. Depending on what to sell as message (promotion), it is wrong for one's emotional or creed to override the public interest. A promoter should sit on the fence by being modest. He should be a little to the right and a little to the left. (Read: "**Words are absolutely powerful**" by the same author)

h) Constantly learning new things to be more creative and retaining the level of fans. The radio station presenter issue illustrated above is an eye opener.

i) Be able to use the latest technological items for promotion. I have seen several vocational study centres whose style of operation is like the formal ones. They wear uniformed dresses with the same style of designs. They must wear uniform footwear and other accessories to the places. Outside the workplace, they may wear choice dresses that suit the occasions. There are shops that are painted with texcote paints with different styles like having shapes of objects in order to look unique and captivating. In the recent, this has been the rave among the shop owners. The accessories in an office are products from the mind of a good promoter. A promoter must be on top of the situation churning out what will make differences in the item being promoted. Good publicist section of government like the minister of information could use his or her office to bring in investors to the nation just as all the public relation, managing the local and foreign desks, in other ministries or private business institutions.

j) Dynamics to make distinguished promotions. When I started to promote my website, I started with friends and families on all social media and mails to just visit, tick like and share with at least a few others in tens. A message of encouragement showing their endorsement is required for others to continue tolling the path. Within a short time, one can imagine the reach of those who have the knowledge of the site as live!

k) Good promoters must avoid simple but costly mistakes. A promoter is not a professor of big words and grammar. The use of lucid words is an ingredient of convincing and unambiguous promotion. A message that is easily decoded by the target encoders should be the working of the promoter. They should be mindful of the fact that they are communicating with the majority of low and moderate level of education. No potential patron of a product or service would find it easy to employ an interpreter before understanding a piece. They would rather buy those ones who messages are clear to understand and interpret.

In general, promotion is eternal and would eternally wear different colours and in different sizes and shapes depending on the nature of the items to be promoted.

1.4 CHANNELS OF PROMOTION: WHAT ARE THE RIGHT TRACKS FOR PROMOTION?

By this, we are looking at placing advertisements and not the countless ways of promotion we have concisely described so far. Advertisements are done either inside the prints or broadcast media. Both involve the use of artisanal skills from different perspectives. In short, the conventional and most popular choice of promotion is the use of media, print, electronic in traditional or digital ways. Many are of the thought and belief that media popularize products and services more than any other ways put together. To this writer, nay. It is never the best channel of promotion. The creativity and versatility to explore each is the determinant of the reach. By experience, we have seen many that have websites whose products are not known to people around their ambience not to talk of those farther away who could be prospective patrons and matrons. The style and the content of the press release sent to hundreds of media station 9print and broadcast combined) of my first work pushed the book to all corners of the world within a short period of time. A promoter should therefore carefully select words and the media to be used in the promotion. The use of wrong and despicable words including the wrong media with bad reputation in the media industry may render the **promotion** fruitless!

Promotion, in view of the above, therefore, has to do with the level of thinking, dynamism and creativity. Promoter must be selective in the choice of media for his product to see the light of the day as anticipated. Never use media with bad reputation not to talk of broadcaster with no affluence in the industry. Media is purposely established for the final products or finished goods ready to be forwarded to the market for procurement by customers. **Promotion**, as earlier narrated in the book, is far beyond this. It has to do telling the target buyers months if not years ahead before the formal release to the market. One can start promotion of a water bottling company from the rainy season through seminars, workshops, talk-shops, for a discussions among others to create suspense and potential buyers at the first day of release. Such books that have created suspense through the writing of reviews on different blogs and media would sell out at the communicated first day of release. Imagine writing a beautifully crafted previews and the comments of the reviewers about the book about three months before formal release, the book would sell out at the day of release! A company can have its **company policy** known to readers of newspapers through the paid interviews at weekends when papers sell most. Through public assessments of the policy, if room is given for suggestions, useful ones may be got free of charge from the respondents that would add values to the policy.

The owners of a business idea must be mindful of the invitees to the formal promotion for the product or service. Just as the classes of people that are invited as contained in the invitation cards would determine how the acceptability such event would be, it would as well tell on the number of attendance at the show. If a school is in need of funds for certain capital project, the success of the ex-colleagues that are attending the alma mater would add values to the event. Such alma mater may enter the headline of newspapers the next day if the members are very important personalities and gurus in their professional careers. The popularity of a club, charity-based organization is known by the social responsibility to better the society where they are located. When the artisans association have their week-long celebration, they wear what they sell. Tailors put on uniform designers to show their works to the public hence creating interest for the locally-made designs and designers in the profession instead of buying the foreign dresses.

OF WHAT RELEVANCE IS 'PROMOTION' TO ANY 'BUSINESS AND INSTITUTIONS'?

Achieving the right result is the purpose of **promotion** on the basis of the nature of economic ideologies and political structures in place. Business that is operating under perfect market competition may have to invest huge sum to promote its goods. Such may spend less under oligopoly situation as there are large number of buyers to have its own market share. No other business is promoted except the only legally recognized by legislation of the government under monopoly situation. In the latter case, whether the manager of such business promote or not, they would have huge patronage. Generally, all 'businesses' target profits with their highly promoted brands. By 'business', we mean all institutions, private and public service, ethnic and religion-based, social clubs and affiliations. In today's world, artistes are used as partners with established beverage companies to build more fans base and hence popularity of the products. Telecom sector used to enter into agreement with educational and service institutions to gear up the sales through popularity. Many are products and services that are promoted through the sponsoring of reality shows, sports, seminars, news headlines, interviews of great personalities, the films and historical documentaries. The research department and sales offices used to identify popular singers, thespians, artists, authors, professionals to be the face of their businesses and institutions. Many a school is named after popular educationists to attract crowds of patrons. In order to promote my books on employment generation, I entered into partnership agreement with different institutions. Both partners derive target objectives from the partnering as promotion expose both brands to the world. Involvement with popular figures in the social media boost the brands of the followers. Charity-based institutions objective is to turn round the situation for better society. And this is the reason for promotion. Sports are promoted to pull crowds of fans who would pay for the souvenirs and tickets. A team is boosted by the talented players in their fold. The unveiling of players at scheduled times is a way of sending the name of the team to the world. On the part of administration, government is seen as business, the 'professional' politicians would say. Manifestoes of the party and the candidates aspiring for a public post must be massively promoted before the electorates could line behind the candidates.

Simply say, the simply listed key areas in the manifestoes which school can read and understand are forms of promoting the candidates to the public (voters). And the gains are- making the huge turn-out of voters, the acceptability or endorsement by the eligible voters by voting massively for the person and the enthronement into office of power. With these, all the paraphernalia of offices are enjoyed having received the political power by the massive votes that surpassed the rest aspirants. The aspirants must have met all prerequisites to be a contender as contain the electoral laws. All the qualities of such aspirants may give an edge over co-contestants in the primaries. And the party would never try to risk a candidate that is not saleable to the people especially the grassroot stakeholders who usually vote personality. As the party must work towards becoming a darling people's party by identifying the actual needs of the people which must be identified in the manifestoes translated in all the languages the voters understand, same must be done by the publicity of the party and media spokesperson of the candidate. If both the party and the aspiring candidates are not adequately promoted, then little will be known about them and this could lead to electoral loss.

On the part of business, rewards of entrepreneurs are huge profits. Many think in the line of making abnormal profits. Before such is attained, marketing of the product or service must have captured millions within the reach first. It is a notion in the selling parlance that a business must target just 10% at most from the number of target customers. By this, a business that targets 100,000 buyers to make anticipated profits must have promoted the products or service to not less than one million prospective customers to have such number as customers. Towards achieving this landmark, a lot of promotion must be done and the promotional tasks must be consistent in order to keep reminding the potential customers of the product. As a business is promoting, others are doing the same substitute and close products in the same market. This is the reason the promotion must go on non-stop till the time of formal release of the product to the market. Makers must therefore be dynamic and in the habits of promoting at all stations. It must not be on a radio station alone but many; not in a television station but many; not in a social media but all; not in the print media alone but all forms of media; not in the books alone but in films. When all these are explored, product or service is registered in the minds of the would-be buyers. And these might have added them in their top-priority list for the month or week the product would be out for consumption.

CHAPTER TWO

2.1. HISTORY OF PROMOTION

"Promotion is about ornaments
Ornaments are assets promoting values and status
Not just values but showing invaluable opportunities"

The history is as old as the creation. Everyone desires to associate with success or a successful personality in order to build a better image (brand). Imagine the reverence someone would have if he is a five and six to a guru in legitimate business or a man of integrity. All the wonders of creations promote the Almighty Omnipotent, Omnipresent and Omniscient that is infinite in Powers to create whatever desires with whatever means and tools at any time and place. Therefore, promotion is an ancient task from the revelations that enjoin man to promote peaceful existence and righteousness. And it can be, without doubt, said that it is old as the creation. By consideration of the reflexes of the word 'promotion so far in the first chapter, 'promotion' could hence be defined to mean the followings: disseminate, propagate, broadcast, share, constant reminder, display, discuss, hype, strategic define, throw open, persistently informing variants of target clients within and outside, hawk, boost, create awareness, sell, market, the contents, the composition, the generic functions, the benefits, the norms, the legacies, the gains, the rewards, the values, the distinguished and real exotic features, the excellent performance or quality, the superiority of a product, service, idea, skill, talent, standard or quality the target users (clients, customers, service beneficiaries, visitors, investors, institutions) would benefit after consumption or use. Every moving creature is displaying the mightiness of God, the Creator. We move around with one thing in mind. We discuss what we have in mind with people. Sometimes, we force our opinions on others. By all these, we are promoting a view, an idea, a concept, a belief... The religion propagators move house to house to share the words of God. The ladies dancing at the streets with customized business uniforms are promoting a product or service, listen to the jingle and their messages. Foreign affairs ministers and government officials used to travel abroad to promote their nation's ideologies on social, economic and political values. No man moves around without a purpose not to talk of emissaries from a nation. Without iota of doubt, the voyage of the white from the advanced nations today to Africa was to discover other places where their economic and political products could be sold. When they had established political structure, they sold their own style of governance to the natives who were under monarchial system of administration. Capitalism was introduced and massively promoted likewise their social values and religion. One can say that directly and indirectly, nations and institutions are promoting one value or the other to prospective buyers or consumers. The environment a business operate and the components influence on such environment would determine the kind of promotion and the manner to go for the promotion. One common feature of all kinds of **promotion** is continuity and consistency with touches of dynamism. It is wrong for a business to stop promotion after recording the first sales, huge or low. It may take some time for the prospective customers to decide to have a taste or a glance to pick interest in the product or item being continually announced to his or her senses. The target clients, regardless of their status, need someone that would continue to remind of the existence and availability of the goods, services, items, ideas, institutions among others. This is a must as competitors are gaining entry into the marketplace every day. Studies of sampled customers of certain product, like Uncle Bens and sardine never know that some of those products that are not available in most retail shops in the country are available in big malls that have modern tastes in infrastructures. And these are the products that were available for all Toms, Dick and Harry at the period of time. They had truly consumed variants of tinned foods and canned drinks from companies abroad in the 70's which have suddenly disappeared in the marketplaces today.

Promotion is an essential of all growth, awareness and development. In short, the creations and creatures in different shapes and sizes are signs showing the Omniscient, Omnipotent and Omnipresent of the Almighty. The sent Prophets of the Almighty is to promote the unequal Might of the Creator. They promote monotheism by their submissive ways of live to the natural laws from the Almighty. They are brands from being model for others to emulate. By their good and righteous morals, we identify the God-sent people. The signs promote the need for synergy for social engineering.

Regalia of office, the mode of palace and the paraphernalia of office distinguish the king from the subjects including the influential people. The palatial mansion of home of the rich distinguishes the wealthy from the indigent. The great warriors were known by the cowries and small gourds-filled wears and other fearful accessories. In many cases, the way they built their houses promoted whom they were.

What about the tribal marks? Different families had different tribal marks to distinguish the people of same ethnic group. Many adopted certain tribal marks to show that they were powerful and opulent.

Another traditional methods of promoting cultural practices is the use of drums, gongs, flute and different dancing steps. Nations with different ethnic groups are known to the nations with distinguished songs, dancing styles and steps, the composition of instruments for typical singers.

The architectural style of residents of ethnic groups differentiates ethnic to ethnic. The northern ethnics in Nigeria built round huts with palm-frond thatch roofs. Those at the southern parts used to have square or rectangular designed mud houses. All these are promoting the level of civilization at the period.

2.2. PROMOTIONAL STRATEGIES IN THE YEARS PAST

History of promotion showed that the style, traditional ones, and the level of cultural interactions have little impact on promotion. The generation of forex from opening up of the tourists sites across the world add life to promotion of all other brands.

Different nations in history including all business and non-business institutions adopted different styles and strategies to promote their products, cultural values, national ideologies and ideas. The stronger nations could impose their cultural values on the conquered territories just as the warring nations of the ages. Sometimes, itinerant traders brought new values to the people met at different places. The possibility that the migrating merchants came across better values was there as they adopted the new values as a replacement for theirs. A good instance is the influence on science, architecture, arts, visual arts, interior decors, book writing (authoring and publishing) and library activities, mode of transactions and transportation and the applications of Mathematics that were post-Quran era in Arabia. And this was the light to the science and technology of different aspects of life in today's inventions and discoveries. (Ref: "**The Bible, The Quran and the modern science**" by the revered French Doctor, Maurice Bucaille) They exchanged these by mutual consent and with interests and not imposition. In the olden days, people used the gong to communicate and called attention to an important issue. Farm produce were sold with cowrie placed on a leaf by its side on the bush path among the Yorubas in the south west Nigeria. The native wears wore at different times were promoting their cultural values. Songs of different sound and lyrics for different seasons were part of the valuable tradition to promote the race.

Later, there was the age of advanced and consistently advancing media when views and ideologies were promoted through local prints. Today, the print industry has gone or developed into online printing. This is unlike the olden days when scripting was the vogue. You communicated with the combination of the vowels and the consonants in the alphabets from certain ethnic group to compose and write letters not long after the discoveries of universal alphabets from different ethnic groups. People who were versatile and knowledgeable on the alphabets became tutors and the writers with the combination of the alphabets. (Ref: "**Words are absolutely powerful**" from the stable of the same author). The founding fathers of the nation created time to write letters and strove to get them printed in the few newspaper in order for their views to reach the public. Many times, lobbying had to be done to ensure a news was on the first page of the newspaper. Unlike today, when a company can afford to advertise their products and services at the front cover page of a newspaper or pop up on mails, social media and blogs from the innovations in the digital media industry.

PROMOTIONAL STRATEGIES IN THE MODERN WORLD

We can examine this under pre-information and communication and technology and after. By after, we mean the ICT era and post-information and communication and technology era. Gone are the days when one covered distance for promotion of a product, service, idea and others. Through well-packaged documentaries from private studios that have the modern communication gadgets, short drama adverts in forms of jingles and interviews could be sent to the popular media station and by this the whole world would be aware of the message being promoted. Video conferencing, live chat, blog or min website, video plus blog called vlog, blog and several ways are products of ICT to promote all things across the nations in different languages. We are in a world where many office-based jobs are done online without much pains except the failure of network in some cases as a possible obstacle.

In the pre-ICT era, as illustrated under the above sub-title, people moved from place to place to have new branches of their businesses. As new people with different orientation migrated, the businesses are proliferated. There is introduction of new technology that would add values to the ones in existence at the new place of settlements. The types of wear and accessories on the migrants could be accepted by the hosts. By this imitation, new values are promoted within the new settlements of the locals and the guests.

During the early time of introducing of the better communication gadgets, people find it useful to use them for communication. Analog radio were used to promote new discoveries to boost agricultural productions instead of sending farm extension workers to farmers at villages that were several miles apart. The development in all facets of professional leanings called for better dissemination of the discoveries and inventions. The communication experts lived up to expectation for the invention of better means of communication to broadcast or promote the new skills and products that would add values to life. By this, the lifespan is boosted and the quality of living standard improved tremendously across the nations that embrace the knowledge and skills. Migrations of people from different nations for green pasture, medical, education or tourism purpose have paved the way for advanced **promotion** of goods and services. Scholarship for students to study at university abroad was a way of exposing the local bred to foreign cultures and values. The gains are for the foreigners as the beneficiaries of the scholarship brought the foreign tastes for foreign foods, clothing, books, electronics, cream, soap and several other essentials of life. Excursions and holding of international symposiums, meetings and conferences at different nations in the world is a way for promoting the host-nation today. This is a reason for the bidding for the intending hosts. In fact, several internal and international politics are involved before hosts are picked. Another major one towards exposing the potentials of a nation to the rest of the world is through the periodical sports events especially football and athletics events. Wise leaders enter into different business pacts and other social issues like students exchange programmes and trainings for any sector of the economy and security forces in order to expose the friends and families of those people to the patronage of their products and services. It is impossible for someone who would stay in a nation for a month to be there with his or her local delicacies and drinks. In the new nation of sojourn, he must buy what they produce there; liked or developed interest in them and could even import the recipe home to publicize to the citizens. At the end, the local people started importation of the foreign goods and services. Without mincemeat of words, this is the foundation of withdrawals from the economy and the need for forex policy to meet the importation needs. Today, billions of dollars are spent by importing nation to meet the imports of the citizens. The economy growth and regression are traced to the consumption of foreign goods. The local production is no more enhanced as people have greater taste for goods from abroad. It is wise for all nations to work on how to grow the local economy especially on imports substitutions in order to lower the demands for forex. Imagine someone from United Kingdom (UK) that bought UK products and valuable cultural values already accustomed to for his people in Nigeria. By so doing, UK products and traditional values have entered homes in the nation. Someone who bought books from another nation has indirectly import cultural values of other races of the world. And the consumption may add to the consumers. Nigerians who have tasted the products may abandon the locally-made ones for preference for the UK product vice versa. It is no more a surprise seeing Nigerian dressing like a Briton vice versa. Promotion sells the new valued assets to the two sides of the world. This is one of the discussed indirect ways of promotion. Ideologies may bring people from across the worlds together and in the course, there would be interests and admiration for opposite values, norms, clothing, foods and drink among others. Imagine the anticipated sales figure of a product or service that is promoted by the actual professionals with years of experience. If experienced chefs adopted a seasoning and proudly promote such with all the indigenous languages and internationally recognized ones, what a huge acceptability it would have in the market. A school that recruited through educational consultants would be able to procure right and competent staff whose contributions to have excellent pupils would eventually promote the school within a short time. This is applicable to all professional service. For employment of the right person for the job, branded consultant, though outsourced, would be right for the recruitment exercise. I could recall of a school that had a problem with the parents who were withdrawing their children from the school. At the time, the popularity of the school was dwindling by the day. To re-energize the school, we worked on we could promote the positive values of the school to the tastes of the parents. We communicated with the staff; re-orientate them; re-organized them; taught how to handle subjects with the use of the modules; and the timetable was re-composed to reflect what we desired for the pupils in terms of excellence especially the core subjects. Within a month of operation, the school wore a new look and the products (pupils) became the pride of the school and the parents. In short, the dented image of the school was laundered and it was promoted beyond the state. The quality of staff in a business environment would promote the objectives as expressly stated in the mission and vision of the institution. We should further to the nation where round peg is put at the round hole. Even, many a nation could see the good sides of an ideology. Contacts of the prophet of Islam with the people all over Arabia turned their idolatry lives into monotheism. Various ways of contacting people and professionals play a major role in the **promotion** of today. The use of ambassadors for a business signed for a number of years has become a new trend in the modern world. Another company may use the phrase 'face of the product'. The institutions may consider a lot of factors to choose who to wear the status of their ambassadors. The latter have ways to portray themselves in the public functions in a way to attract more fans to the ones that pave the way for their emergence as the ambassadors. If a footballer has 100m followers on a social media, such brand can advertise and win sales for a product. Such a person has become an idol of sort. If he or she presents a product or service for his fans on the same media, then the product or service has high tendency to sell to over 10 million from the ardent followers of the star player.

As dynamics in the modern world continue to change with different tides and waves of life, the promotion of different things grow. In fact, there are one thousand and one ways to promote a particular issue. If I have an opinion to share with American President, I can go to the internet to put my opinion on email box for perusal. Business owners can use telephone to present their products or services to customers or clients. A bulk short message service can reach millions with a click of the button. The same with the use of email to spread a message with a little cost. Video-conferencing is at the comfort of the users and all forms of promoting a product or service is cheaply done. Unlike in the past when logistics environment could render the sending of message a hectic task. In the villages before the advancement in the information and communication technology, people write letters. Executive in offices relied so much in official letters to send memos to their employees at their point of service. One of the best ways to communicate is to use telegram.

CHAPTER THREE

3.1 PROMOTION AND TECHNOLOGY

From the vast discussion under the last sub-chapter, the evolution in Information Technology has impacted greatly (positively) on promotion. Simply say, technology innovations and devices have added bigger values to the world of promotion in all sense of the word. It is easy to demonstrate to the world how a product works under a few minutes with uploading on popular social media. Many films are uploaded on twitter and the likes to attract viewers across the world. Many a popular singers is known after reaching out to prospective fans online. With technology, one can run mobile office without stress. Instead of risking travelling, telemedicine, online banking and online tutorial among several other online services are done very cheap to the users. It is easy for those who do not have the time for shopping to shop and buy online. It takes the sellers and makers to promote their ware online for a charge or under an agreement with the e-market place to meet their target in sales and profits. Elegant lady that is into modelling business, though not permissible in the monotheistic religions, can be seen throughout the world of internet especially if such catwalks with designers being promoted are on beamed to viewers live.

3.2 PROMOTION AND ARTS

Artworks are generally believed to be the major contents that promote a people by ethno-religion background, an institution and professions. Individuals that are endowed with skills in artworks are mostly called artisans. In all spheres of live, especially in the environments, are the works of arts. Through the art groups, entertainment industry proliferate and nations have made gains from the exposure of the talents-based arts. We can rightly say that art is innate talent that is transferable to others who are interested to learn the arts. In the northern

Nigeria, the artworks on the hides and skins were the employment generator for the weavers and makers of shoes and bags including certain utensils. Visual artworks are employed as part of promoting a business in today's world. Visit homes and offices to appraise the works from arts. Offices especially financial institutions used to occupy the walls with different accessories to beautify the working inner rooms for staff members and the target guests who are the customers. Most used to cover the walls with beautiful paints with stylish touches and the florists attractions and creativity. The interior decors are incomplete without the casting on marbles, the tilling of the floors, the visual artists showing different expression, the working fittings among others that would say 'keep coming, dear customers'. The cool welcoming voices of the beautiful damsels and smartly dressed members of staff is enough attraction of people of different personalities to the banks for different services. Landscaping of towns would add values or promotion to a sleeping town and nation at corners to be a force to be reckoned with. Trees along the highways is another way of promoting the nation. Good roads that connect the countryside to the hinterland is an added value promoting a nation. All entertainers add spices to events and boost the tourist attractions to the nation. Supporting the major actors who are so endowed shall be a good path to promote the national values. Visit all banks and other financial institutions; visit many companies around you and homes of people, different aesthetics from innate arts have become part and parcel of the decors in every structure. Towards creating serene environment where services are rendered, where people can relax and talk business, interior decors from the works of art are inevitable.

No customer who visited such institutions with visual artworks would cease from coming for business transaction again.

Like banks, like the hospitality business owners; aesthetics attract people to find home away from home for relaxation. A beehive place for such is a place well promoted and attractive. A hotel, park, garden and the likes would be the right choice for relaxation of the people, regardless of the affiliations, age, faith and gender, provided there are what it takes to have serene atmosphere for relaxation and enjoyment.

3.3 PROMOTION AND SERVICES

A quality service needs to be known to the public. Passers-by would admire to be informed about the services that would quench their thirsts. Customers or clients desire to enjoy satisfactory service at the comforts of their homes and offices. This is doable if found within their jurisdiction. A catalyst is that all services that target patronage must be properly promoted. A piece of advice for all service providers read- 'Please, go extra mile if you intend to make impact on your choice of profession' as business-minded professional and motivators would say. People and institutions are always in need of service for certain activity. It is onus on the service providers to go extra mile to appeal to the minds of the target clients via taking different steps. We have discussed how business environmental aesthetics would catch the interests of would-be customers to a service; the first step is therefore to ensure clean and tidy (organize) is a bait to attract clients to trickle into the business premises for service. Other areas should include enjoy maximum comforts with low fees as charge. By this, we mean, provide quality service delivery in order to enjoy free publicity from satisfied clients if you are targeting volumes of patronage. The quality of service should be measurable with the affordable service charge in money. The corporate dressing and the politeness of the well-trained staff is a way of promotion the station.

In view of the points made above, advertisement is major. If your service is unknown, move round to sell the message. A radio station is set to compete with several public and private owned station in the city. What did the management of the station do? They recruited star presenters from different stations to do the same jobs at the station. With this, all the fans of the star presenters became the fans of the new station. If a promoter is assigned to promote a new concept in service sector. Such must do his homework right to identify the service by source and the need for the service. There is the need to move ahead of the stakeholders who are in the market before it. Picking some fantastic areas of public interests and adding these features to the newly designed concept would sell the service. If I want to promote a media station, I shall repackage the old contents to wear a modern look towards capturing the large fans base seeking for modernity. The use of rave of the moment in songs and concepts such as the fusion of entertainment, fashion with the concepts shall be a focus. No programme would come on air without entertaining and fashion flavours. Each time I passed by electronic billboards that are not operated or close early. Several things come to my mind. The managers are bereft of promotion ideas. It is as simple as that. I intentionally delved into how makers of products and the providers of services could generate huge sales through making new customers and retaining the old ones. One of the major challenges that they face is how to go about promotion. All businesses, individuals that are brands, all government and private owned institutions need quality publicists with modern training and orientations about promotion. As a promoter or publicist, keep learning new relevant skills by mixing or relating with people and institutions of different approaches and orientations. Socialize and keeping asking when you are at cross roads in order to be effective, efficient and remain focused on the job for those who seek or in need your service. As far as human being exists, services are needed by different people. When housing units are occupied, there is need for maintenance by all professionals in building technology. There are jobs from artisans to manage the homes from dilapidation. Hawk the service through the estate managers or the civil engineers that built them. Move to the housing estates that own the homes. Go to ministry of housing to secure maintenance jobs.

3.4 **PROMOTION AND PRODUCTS**

In the course of this work, we have made a sample of the approach the author employed in the selling of his book. This is applicable to all other forms of promotion for different items. Products, no matter the quality and the vastness of the prospective clients or customers, must be adequately promoted.

Without doubt, zeroing promotion down to product and service of the profit and not-for-profit institutions, there is dire need for promotion. And quality products and of service is worthy of celebration and promotion. No mother would hide her beautiful baby. No woman of pretty figure would like to be at the back. Everyone likes to display the quality he is made up of. Products that have been tested and received positive assessments cannot be hidden. In the departmental stores, attractive products are placed at open places for customers to see. It is wrong to employ the service of an introvert sales representative to manage a shop or an office. The psychology of the sales agents and the receptionists or the secretary play a great role in the popularity and possible patronage of an item. A promoter must never employ such personality as part of the team. The next step is to procure such machines and facility that would drive the popularity to the target numbers of audience wherever they are found or located at a particular point in time. In this ICT era, the involvement of all facilities from the ICT industry must not be ignored. The search engine optimization (SEO) displays the product by the number of search in popularity. In most cases, do not rely on free sites as they may never render you the promotion you seek. Try to start promoting with the nest eggs or the crowd fund that is at your disposal to start promotional activities. Start growing your fans base and possible clients gradually. A quality product or service has its first attraction from the title. As a promoter, start from the title and the sub-titles, if there is need for your own type of product. Never promote a product or service that is fake or hidden under multi-purpose. Most multi-purpose products, by close observations at different times and places, end up to be substandard that would never serve the generic functions. Investigate thoroughly what you are intending to promote. There are manufacturers who used to give nicknames to their products in order to be more acceptable to other segments of customers. Imagine calling a beverage 'gbogbonise' meaning 'all-purpose' or 'multipurpose' as nickname, this may attract several other people beyond the major targets in the markets.

The manufacturers and sellers, staff and private, must understand all the generic functions of a product before such enters the market for promotion. There is possibility for target customer to ask questions about the product, for such to be accepted by people, sellers must be able to find answers to all questions in a very sincere and logical way that would attack the reasoning of the public.

Limitless are the ways to promote products and services by the producers. The type of promotion for such depends on the nature, norms, values by faith, affiliation, association, ideology of the target customers in the environment. It is possible for a maker to use different languages, bilingual or multilingual for promotion. The illiterate traders in the market for the presentation of the goods or services. Sometimes, products or service for toddlers could be promoted with animation and cartoons. Brand in brand could make positive impact on the acceptability (by sales) of products of the producers. We have seen beverage brands that are sold with free recharge cards. School kits are sold with free educational materials. Shoes and designers are sold with free perfume.

PROMOTION AND GLOBAL DEVELOPMENT

All nations in the world must have a list of values and assets that must be promoted to attract investors from within and outside. Nations must however must not promote hate speeches and related. The citizens must not commit xenophobic attacks with impunity. Studies show that most nations are pluralistic environment. By pluralistic, we mean that they are multi-ethnics and multi-religions. In another clime, they are multi-party nations with different political and economic ideologies. Understanding the ideologies on the economy and ethno-religion are significant in a way to promote the contents to other worlds. The United Nations special days for different commemoration are focused on promotion of values domiciling in those nations. Let us look at an instance. The world cultural day is commemorated for nations to celebrate all the list of cultural artefacts, festivals and the local technology products of the people of different races and faiths. Through the promotion and celebration of local arts and cultural values, most of the nations may not have trade imbalance again as more of the local produce shall be patronized and consumed hence reducing the tastes for imports from outside.

Generally, the gains, of promotion of values of each nation of the world, are the increasing of employment generation through huge local patronages, the soaring of the gross national income and increased per capita income for better standard of living.

In order to avoid loss of patronages, multi-purpose products are becoming a thing of the past. Promoters would promote a product that would serve a particular value in order to retain his integrity as a brand and credible (reliable) promoter.

CHAPTER FOUR

4.1 WHAT ARE THE GAINS OF PROMOTIONS TO BUSINESS AND INSTITUTIONS?

We have discussed how promotion of culture through different measures determining all the conditions of economies in the world. In addition, the open up of nations through visa free to nations is a way to sell the values and products of those nations to the visitors. Many people came back home to establish English curriculum-based schools. Many Chinese restaurants are proliferating simply as a result of cultural values imbibed at the meeting points. Without doubt, the promotion of valuable products and services from other nations have increased the gains of the bigger nations. Examples are countless. Think over the types of clothes and designers you wear in your nation. What about the toilet soaps and creams you use?

Simply say, all forms of promotion target recording huge patronage and ends in huge sales for target profits for the business. It boosts the acceptability and creates new customers adding to the existing ones. Through promotion, brand is created from brand. New brands that are created from existing brands also become a brand that would create other brands and the process is eternal. What do we mean? If scouts discover football talents in a field of play, and all necessary exposures are given the talent to become a star, such scouts have become brands in the scouting profession also. In a team of players, some football talents that could through their natural ingenuity change the tempo and win games would turn the rest into stars. Imagine all the players of Real Madrid football club that had won eleven Champions cup in Europe, a few popular stars like Portuguese Cristiana Ronaldo, Brazilian Marcelo, Spanish Sergio Ramos, Welsh Gareth Bale among others in the team create new brands in others. Many barely unknown players in the winning team have also become stars in Europe and the football world. Those who sell the products and services of others could become brand sellers if they beat the target and recognized for the feat.

Good and vocal readers of books, news could become a brand presenters on radio and television. Many fans of media stations become household names as a result of right interpretations of concepts and contents as packaged by the programme director. Directly and indirectly, product or service could be promoted by free publicists especially the satisfied customers. On the other way, a dissatisfied customer could render a brand non-appealing to potential buyers in the market. Many times, the ardent fans, the friends, families and kind neighbours of the brand owners celebrate and promote the product or service to generate more customers. Freebies to school children by companies may create interests of families to the procurement of the commodity. Promotion of basic needs like education, health, community development make gains for the business in the increasing of the all-time patronage. The piece of advice is that 'use your intelligence to turn yourself into a brand. Never be jealous of achievement of another, you are on the part to become a star if you promote the star brand. The noblest man that was sent as mercy to all creatures was reported to have said 'sitting at the blacksmith shop would render the person to smell like the smith'. Use the light of others to walk the right path. Many nations of the world are promoted by their nationalist singers, film makers, authors, newspapers, broadcasters, erudite scholars, dedicated professionals use their professional leaning to boost the image of the nation vice versa. A popular singer in Nigeria visit to Disney world in Florida, America fetched him the honourary doctorate degree for releasing song that promote the wonders in the Disney world. Many poor traders have their business customized and got free promotional kits from telecoms for being at the right location.

Generally, business environments and institutions that are positively promoted would improve the viability and the profitability of all businesses vice versa.

OF WHAT RELEVANCE IS PROMOTION TO A GOVERNMENT?

The first poser is 'what does government need to promote? Of course, government must promote its policies and institutions. The national economic blueprint shown in the policy formulated by each of the sectors boost the brand of the nation. Such enabling incentives must also be promoted to attract foreign direct investments and boost the gross domestic products hence income and per capita income.

The second poser is 'how best should government make the **promotions**?' Each institution where policies are formulated must be headed by popular brands in official. An institution with seasoned professionals who had garnered wide experience on the job would be the brand that would transfer brand to the institution. Let us support this by analogy. If government intends to promote the oil sector, it needs to build the management around experienced and revered professionals on oil industry. With this, the sector has also become focus of the stakeholders in the industry.

The third poser remains: "What is the relevance of promotion?" Just as the gains for individuals and institutions, following are the gains of promotion:

a) Exposure of the nation to the world in order to attract foreign direct investments and boost the economy

b) Creating revenue-employment opportunities for the nation to improve the standards of living

c) To enhance the aesthetics of the nation

d) To earn deserve respect from all other sovereign nations and independent institutions.

WHAT DOES PROMOTION MEAN TO OTHER FACETS OF LIFE-ECONOMY, THEOLOGY, IDEOLOGY..?

As a matter of fact, everyone that professes an ideology, faith or others must is a promoter of such. This is the reason why man must live by standard laid down by the bloc such belongs. Muslims should dress like a Muslim. Every faith should be proud to promote the values and norms of their faiths without molestation. Ethnic should cherish their cultures by promoting what inherent in the cultural values. A socialist by economy ideology should be proud of being one and the practice of the ideology should be total provided it does not infringe on the right of others who share different ideology. It is the natural will of the Creator that we are not created one race according to the incorruptible scripture. Man is of different races and of different attitudes. What a Muslim by birth value, as a human being born into a parent with contradictory cultural values, may contradict what the religion anticipates from him. To be devout one, he has to sacrifice his interest for the tenets of the religion to prevail and this attitude makes him a Muslim he professes and acting.

CHAPTER FIVE

5.1. WHAT ARE THE CHALLENGES FACING PROMOTION?

This is purely business operating environment. The political and economic with recognition of the ethno-religion values play major role in the promotion of products, services, resolutions, ideologies among others. Challenges against promotion takes different ways. Some of them are:

a) **IDEOLOGICAL DIFFERENCE AND FRICTIONS**: Nations are blessed with people with different ideologies of faith, political affiliations. There is no unity of ideology and making it difficult to have united national values to be promoted. Most leaders are in the habit of patronizing mainly foreign countries. Some are as bad as importing everything for building and by so doing billions are withdrawing from the economy.

b) **ETHNIC VARIANTS**: Each of the ethnic groups in nations has variants of cultural values and norms that are abandoned for foreign tastes and values. Many ethnic groups have replaced their local foods with foreign ones, local drugs for the orthodox medicine at a larger percentage among others. If the business adopts a promotional act that are against certain ethnic, such brand being promoted may have a setback in terms of target success. There are ethnic groups that do not desire to have anything to do with others vice versa for unfounded flimsy excuses and reasons.

c) **PARENTAL INFLUENCE**: Parents who are so interested in foreign dialects, foreign goods and services would impose this on the children directly and indirectly. Their children would be sent to foreign schools where their native languages are not spoken. At home, they do not chat with the dialects with the children. The children are not exposed to the local foods and drugs. They don't listen to traditional songs not to talk of watching the local films. Indirectly, the parents in the category have replaced their heritage with foreign values.

d) **MEDIA INFLUENCES**: In nations after colonialism when media stations were more popularized, the contents from the tube that broadcast to every home become the mode of throwing aside the traditional values gradually as a larger percentage of the contents being promoted from entertainment to the news often broadcast on air are sufficiently flavoured by the foreign culture in language, mode of dressing, the placed adverts of foods in cans and bottles, the civilization of the west among others. Media is expected to boost local contents but contrary is the case.

e) **PERSONAL EGO**: Individuals, though from different ethnic group and ideologies, may have different perceptions about life and therefore may or may not be interested in a particular promotion style of any local-based contents. Many, as a result of personal ego, prefer promoting foreign contents at the peril of the local content waiting for promotion. To these mind, the foreign ones are of quality while the home-made are inferior by assessment. We have seen employees of certain firms that do not patronize the products and services being produced from the factory or the service stations where they work. Their activities are always against the institutions they are part and parcel. People from different professional leanings must be patriotic to design different practicable ways to promote the national values.

f) **FAILURE TO HAVE COLLECTIONS OF BRANDS AND ITEMS TO PROMOTE**: institutions and nations patronize items from abroad. We have seen situations where manpower (even artisans) are recruited abroad. I have been to school in the course of promoting our books to the school where the secretary opened up that the proprietress was in the habit of importing all textbooks from the nations abroad. She did not have flair for the local publishers and the authors. How would such school produce pupils that would have interest to be proud of the ethnic values and culture? Visit private libraries and you would be astounded seeing the shelves filled up with foreign books. Check the inner part of the cover page of some textbooks, you would find out that they were published abroad at the expense of the publishing factories within. Institutions and nations that are lagging behind in the promotion of all the business and other valuable items from within do not have reliable statistical data to work with. It is doable if a nation has records up to date vice versa.

g) **LACK OF QUALITY MANPOWER**: Quality manpower is a pillar to develop all facets of live- education, medical, financial, construction and all other social services. Nations whose educational institutions, even the non-formal education institutions, fail to churn out quality manpower for the purpose of promoting home-grown values may not grow at anticipated rate. Such may be underdeveloped for a long time. The touch of quality people managing different institutions would have added values to promotion in all ramifications but it is otherwise at the absence of manpower.

h) **LACK OF TRUST**: There is no mutual trust among the people and institutions. The reason may be out of envy where an ethnic looks down on the cherished values of the other. Many ethnics do not have trust in those at the helms who are from another descent or ethnic group. This is common where tribal bitter politics are done without remorse. It is a nation where certain ethnic groups are living as second citizens. Instead of collating the multi-ethnic values to become national assets to be promoted, they become otherwise.

i) **SLOW BUREAUCRACY:** Most of the low developing nations always have problem of unpatriotic elements working in the offices. Graft has been a major factor. Studies show that workers rate of performance are always high at the earlier time of recruitment. As they grow in age and spending more time, their services (productivity) go down south. It is common in the public offices. The private institutions used to maintain their company ethics guiding against slow job.

j) **LACK OF ADEQUATE INFRASTRUCTURES**: Any institution, business or charity-based, including the nation that does not have adequate social infrastructures is not worthy for visitors who could be the ones that would import direct investments to the nation. The insufficiency of working infrastructures would never attract the anticipated investors and tourist.

k) **LACK OF SECURITY**: Most nations that are developed never play idle with the security of the nations. The reverse is the case with the poor nations that are lagging behind. A nation that is not secure is badly promoted in the comity of nations.

l) **LACK OF VISIONARY LEADERS**: It takes leaders who share the vision about promotion of national assets and values that would key into the aspect. Unfortunately, how many of the poor nations reason along several ways we have rolled out to showcase the good things that are brands?

m) **POLICY**: They are either internal or external. Inconsistent policies from the institutions and leaders at different positions of authorities are not working for promotion of a business and institutions for the benefits of the national economic growth and development. As aforementioned, the imbibe of the culture of issuing free visa and scholarships for indigenes from other nations, the bid to host different seminars and symposiums including sport events are roadmap to attract patronage from this style of promotion. Imagine the ban of using certain cosmetics or gender in the promotion of a work to the target customers or clients. Though, the policy is designed by the selected administrative plans on the sectors. There may be national policy that protect the local products and services which would lead to the ban of promoting the foreign imports in the media stations across the nation.

n) **BUSINESS ENVIRONMENT**: Unhealthy promotion that is not regulated by the relevant authority may render promotion of another competitive or substitutes to be out of circulation. A situation where the big investors use freebies that the smaller investment can never afford is an unhealthy to the business environment. It does give room for the other business to breathe.

o) **DEARTH OF THINK TANKS**: it is established that foreign nations used different freebies to expose the local people and brands to their own brands and values. What stop the think tanks within to do likewise and create ways they can attract those from abroad to the nation?

p) **LACK OF VERSATILE AND CREATIVE PUBLICIST**: In all spheres of life, there must be publicists of good values. In institutions, the public relation offices must be up and doing. In public offices, the publicists are the spokespersons that divulge and analyse the workings of government. All cannot be the publicists at the same time to avoid acting parrot. In a situation where quality publicist is available, it will be a great challenge to the family, ethnic, faith, institution, government et al for their voices to be heard.

5.2 HOW BEST TO TACKLE THE CHALLENGES HEADLONG?

The listed challenges of promotion at the previous sub-section must first be critically examined objectively analysed particularly as related to a particular form of promoting item or issue. And these challenges vary from place to place, institution to institution and ideology to ideology. In short, the reverse of the challenges are the solutions to tackle them headlong. Below are some:

a) **IDEOLOGICAL DIFFERENCE AND FRICTIONS:** Institutions and nations that are ruled by the elites who are the products of foreign universities used to embrace foreign ideologies than be proud of the local contents. Institutions and nation should treat the ideological differences by having a convergent point in order to promote the local contents to avoid losing quality manpower and huge sum abroad. Nation, institution and others should have this to avoid friction and conflicting interests.

b) **ETHNIC VARIANTS**: There must be proper and undoubtable understanding of what could promote a product, service, institution and others. An announcer of a product or service must toll the path of modesty. Studying the pros' and cons' that would enhance avoid stepping on toes.

c) **PARENTAL INFLUENCE:** Promote good virtues even if your parents are against this stand. Parents must live as true role model in the promotion of family-lineage values and embracing the national values. A model and teacher of good virtues must patiently teach others the same by writing, acting and speaking the virtues at all times and places. In most cases, parents may rely on past experience to be mending the children and this may have negative effects on the children, the society they live and the nation. Imagine a parent that combines idolatry ritual worship with those in the places of worship of any monotheistic religions. Such must be intelligently corrected to sieve the attitude from the dictates of the faiths. Two contradicting things should be promoted.

d) **MEDIA INFLUENCES**: The concepts and contents of the media-based programmes must be censored before such are broadcast to the public. Sociologists are of the believe that media has greater influence than those of the parents and institutions. The regulatory institutions must do this in a way to check possible wrong promotion of product, services, institutions, events among others that are permissible to be promoted.

e) **PERSONAL EGO**: One should be able to control one's self-ego to override the efforts to promote what we have on ground. A media-based professional must not allow his or her personal emotion to have negative influence on what is presented and packaged to be produced for audience. By personal ego, we include the self-interests that could be ethno-religion flavoured. Such must not have ideological interests.

f) **FAILURE TO HAVE COLLECTIONS OF BRANDS AND ITEMS TO PROMOTE**: Nations, institutions and individuals must have the real information about the brands for promotion. When the MDAs secure the lists of the items to be produced, the promotion would be on top gear.

g) **LACK OF QUALITY MANPOWER**: Enough manpower from different and relevant institutions must be available at the right places to prevent wrong announcements. It does not worth it to have incompetent medical teams in the hospitals. It is wrong for incompetent engineers be awarded building contracts.

h) **LACK OF TRUST**: Trust is an ingredient to build all nations and institutions. A nation that is known with integrity shall enjoy free positive publicity. The character evaluation and the sensitization of what would bring about integrity to the nation and the institutions including individuals must be a watchword.

i) **SLOW BUREAUCRACY:** Since slow bureaucracy is a clog in the wheel of progress of a nation even private institutions, there is need to put in place friction-free bureaucracy for easy flowing of information and documents.

j) **LACK OF ADEQUATE INFRASTRUCTURES**: Infrastructures are vital to promote a nation to investors and tourists. All nations in the world that are advanced made working infrastructures top priority. The nationals and the foreigners find quality infrastructures inevitable to reduce cost of production. This is a lesson for the underdeveloped economies of the world. The nature of landscape and the ever-clean environment of nations in Europe and North America has been attraction of the people of diverse culture around the world. By the heavy migration, all the cultural values of the nations have been promoted to the migrants.

k) **LACK OF SECURITY**: Security must be a major agenda for the government, private institutions and individuals to enable promotion of right values. Tourist of investors shall find a secure place right business environment for their investments. A secured community and institutions that have safety-first as motto shall be a worthy place for visitors. A mentor told me the reason investors prefer America and Europe for investments despite the high criminal rate. He bared his mind based on his personal experience while living at that part of the world. 'if you are robbed at gunpoint, do not fight the criminal. Just go and report at the nearest police station. There is surveillance camera whose footage shall capture the scene and the criminal would soon be arrested and prosecuted. In short, your lost asset shall be returned to you the moment the criminal is caught within a short time to the time of the incident'. This revelation pushed me into deep researching and writing of another explicit book titled *"**Understanding Business Environment, right or wrong**"*)

l) **LACK OF VISIONARY LEADERS**: Social think tanks at the seats of power are inevitable for the emergence of visionary leaders in some cases.

m) **POLICY:** If a policy does not promote certain positive values, then there must be revision and updating. Business institution, public administration and individuals must review policies that would promote the right values.

n) **BUSINESS ENVIRONMENT**: Without doubt, enabling environment used to face hard task to come by. And the making of right business environment differs from nation to nation. All items and facilities that are found to be right in a nation may never work in the other. It is onus on each institution, individual, town and nation to identify the actual provision to be made to promote them into limelight as anticipated.

o) **DEARTH OF THINK TANKS**: Modernity demands for modern touches of promotion. I was passing by a fashion designing shop whose interior decors from stylish painting really attract every potential clients. The style of architecture where red bricks were used to build the round huts serving as classrooms really dropped my jaws when I entered at the school premises. I believed that the two places enjoyed right thinking think tanks. To promote a city from slum, the urban planning and the type of architectural designs shall be a way to promote the place.

p) **LACK OF VERSATILE AND CREATIVE PUBLICIST**: In all three, there must be a leader chosen by the three so admonished the noblest sent to all creatures. The spokesperson is speaking the interests of others. Such has been empowered to lead them in talks. The lead voice must be vocal, charismatic, highly exposed and highly knowledgeable. Publicist could also be multi-lingual to penetrate a large audience wherever they are found. A creative publicist must be one with a right approach. The use of right and suitable words could be the best way to promote cherished values.

5.3 WHAT OTHER INPUTS ARE NEEDED TO IMPROVE ON PROMOTION?

We can categorize these under characters of man which are the followings:

a) **TOLERANCE**: To promote a product or service as a business-oriented person, recognize all segments of people by tolerating them in the use of language and dressing. Be neutral to avoid being sentimental. Choose the right words and keep mute when you are frustrated.

b) **TRANSPARENCY**: No customer that was deceived the first time would patronize such product the next time. Once bitten, they say, twice shy.

c) **FOCUS**: Be objective. Every individual must set out the right paths to promote issues. We should be religiously focused. Always think over what would make the item being promoted difference in the market.

d) **CLEAR DEFINITION**: There should be clear information about the items to be positioned to the public eye. The mode of scripting the jingles for a product cannot be the same for services. Also, the style of promotion to attract investors in enabling environment differ from sector to sector. The tools of promotion must be unambiguously defined and stated.

e) **CONSISTENCY**: It is defined as 'never relenting'. Let people and institution know you by what you are doing in the name of promotion. Be an ambassador of the item you are promoting. Wear the logo and trademark with pride. Never hesitate to use the product you are passionately promoting. Never fail to recommend the material to others at all places. Showing special interests and loyalty

f) **PERSUASSION**: The target people and institutions should be continually persuaded via moral encouragement to continue their patronage.

5.4 BRAINSTORMING GENERAL EXERCISES ON PROMOTION

a) Authors need professional books reviewers, literary agents, copy editors, popular media-print and electronics, social media, brand publishers, popular independent marketers among others to popularize their intellectual property. The film producers also need reviewers, popular bloggers and digital sites, box office, and others to promote the films. The digital technology business owners and the media stations are in need of established content managers, professional developers and web designers, software producers among others to promote the business. List those the following need to promote the brands:

i) Legal practitioners

ii) Engineers

iii) Accountants

iv) Teachers

v) Thespians

vi) Politicians

vii) Administrators

viii) Manufacturers

ix) A selected-named service station

x) Independent service providers (Select a choice service)

CHAPTER SIX

PROMOTION AND POLITICAL INSTITUTIONS

From the chapter four, we desire to expand the scope of the relationship between promotion and the political institutions. We would look at the promotion of political manifestoes and their aspirants to be sold to the electorates. All political parties must have logo, the brand name and sub-title that must be political slogan. For instance, a political party in Nigeria has 'power to the people' as the slogan of the party and a symbol depicting protection for the people under the party and the citizens of the nation. In some cases, the trademark slogan and the symbols in the flag and other insignia of the founding fathers depict the vision and mission to be participant in the political atmosphere. Unfortunately, many eligible voters never care for what the list of symbols stand for. They vote the candidate and not the party. The institution does not stop after assuming the seat of power. There is need for further promotion of economic blueprints and the enabling policies for the growth and development of the economy. The political relevance of the nation must be constantly promoted to boost the political ties and foreign mission.

PROMOTION AND ETHNO-RELIGION VALUES

Religion crises could be averted at all nations provided right methods of promotion are undertook on the norms and ethics of the institutions by the authority. Unhealthy promotion in the use of degrading and blasphemous languages are not applicable in the propagation of a religion ethics and values. Tolerance should be promoted by all religions to foster synergy and unity. All ethnic groups must communicate the right values to the other people from different ethnic groups. This could be done by the constant use of ethnic accessories, speaking the local dialect over foreign ones, eat the local foods, cherish the traditional forms of entertainment always. Set up processes of promoting and championing the traditional values. The same is applicable to the religion. Every faithful should be proud to worship his religion at the right place without compromising any of the teaching and practices. By being fundamental, and not extremism, is promoting the right tenets of the faith.

PROMOTION OF ECONOMIC INSTITUTIONS

The economic institutions deserve to be promoted by the external and internal institutions hence the target beneficiaries could understand how they can benefit from the provision. Many are ignorant of the facilities that are in the books of financial institutions especially the government-owned banks. The kind of economic ideologies adopted by a nation would decide the limitations to promotion. Some economic policy may not allow the promotion of certain products and services. As revealed in the course of this work, it is prohibited to promote alcohol and pork in the nation where Islam is the dominant religion of the majority and Islam is a state religion. For a business to thrive in a nation, there must be critical examination of the religion and ethnic values of the people after all, the people chose their leaders and the socio-economic and the political ideologies being used to administer the nation. In the economic ideological parlance, no situation in the market support neglect of promotion to meet the target. All profit-oriented business whether in oligopoly, monopoly and perfect market competition must continue to promote in order to attract the right size and shapes of customers at right places at a given or set time. Having a few sellers does not mean that customers would troop in trickles to patronize a product or service. The customers must be able to be convinced by the selected chosen words of promotion. Charity-based institutions must communicate what they have in stores gratis to the target patrons.

PROMOTION AND OTHERS

All facets of life particularly the positive ones that would add values to life must be promoted. Celebrate good people. Rewards excellence. Give due recognition. Promote to the next levels as and when due. Reward efficiency and virtues with promotions and material rewards. Promote the environments with floral landscape and different aesthetics. We are promoting one thing or the other whether we are remunerated or not. At least, we live in a house built by certain brand in civil engineering. We wear clothes that are designed by a brand in designers. We wear foot wears that are products of some brand. Do not promote what would have infringements to the right of others. We eat foods and drinks produce by brands. In all forms of promotions, modesty is a must. The noblest sent to all creatures taught 'modesty is a half of faith'.

EPILOGUE

Promote right values at the right time
Watch what you say
Mind the manner of dressing
Watch what you write, you authors
Watch your costumes, you thespians and entertainers
Speak right, you the publicists
Choose the positive words, you the activists and critics
Never speak propagandas and fabrications, you priests
Respect and act the duties of your office
Never be arrogant and deceive by paraphernalia of office
People watch you and admirers embrace your acts
Walk the talk to promote the right values
Write sense to promote right values
Employ the right economy that can be imbibed
Never impose what would affect nation and nationals positively

We are all promoters
In all positions we are
At every institution we are
Whatever associations and affiliations we are
The mission and vision must be promoted
Doing the right promotion with passion, a must
And the impact on the nations is tremendous"

ABOUT THE BOOK

The author looked beyond the use of promotion to sell a product to target buyers or consumers. He research deeply into all aspects of life that are promoted directly and indirectly. He dealt with the business promotion that is mostly attached to economy in business parlance as a platform to unveil all other ways of promoting values from different perspectives.

In business parlance, he is of the school of thought that agrees on the statement thus 'one of the four major marketing mix is PROMOTION. The salient questions are: What do we promote? How do we promote? Where do we promote? When do we promote? The questions are not just for products and services. By the incisive revelations in the book, the author, researched into different issues across the boards that need promotion at all times through the use of right medium of communication. One may ask "How do we promote our nation and national values? How do we promote our ethno-religion values? How can we promote our institutions and local foods and drinks? How would parties promote their manifestoes and the aspirants?

The book is a purely motivational book that guides all crops of professionals on how to announce their products or services; ethnic and national values; associations and affiliations' political and socio-economic features among others in any form to the world of customers. Asking who this book is meant for? Of course, every professional in the private and public service must have copies for distribution for others to learn why and how they should go about promotion with time demands. The book is highly recommended for the manufacturers, service providers, the leaders at government ministries, department and agencies, the jobs seekers, the independent sales agents, sales representatives, mentors, motivational speakers, teachers, political ideologists and strategists among others. The content would guide them into high level of productivity.

ABOUT THE AUTHOR

He is a prolific writer, researcher, think tank, child educationist of repute, motivational speaker, seminar presenter, socio-economic and political activist. He is the author of the research-based books that are popular in the online markets. Some of his hit entrepreneurship books are 'Jobs with zero capital'; Creating new jobs from the existing jobs; Being my own boss- a sequel to 'Creating new jobs from the existing jobs; wastes to wealth jobs; others on economics and administration include Economic recession, the trends, the causes, the spiral effects and the practicable solutions; Piracy, the trends, the spiral effects and the practicable solutions; Winning huge sales and increasing clients base; Understanding business environment, right or wrong; those on art and philosophy include "Words are absolutely powerful"; The naked truths; Ajelende (an adaptation of 'Think within'), Safiya, the heroine died among others.

He, as the Director of Research, Addin Resources Ventures, is a socio-economic think-tanks whose mission is the proffering practicable solutions to all challenges facing mankind on the leverage of producing manpower for even development of all nations.

He is a product of the citadel of technological innovations, The Polytechnic Ibadan with diploma in Business administration, from Alapa family and married with children.

www.ingramcontent.com/pod-product-compliance
Lightning Source LLC
Chambersburg PA
CBHW020451220526
45464CB00002B/951